INSIDE THE SAUCERS

BY TIMOTHY GREEN BECKLEY
Mr. UFOs Teenage Years!

With Additional Material by: Allen Greenfield, Gene Steinberg, David Halperin, Rick Hilberg, Brad Steiger, Edward J. Babcock, Jerome Clark, Kenneth L. Larson, George D. Fawcett

Color Rendering By: Carol Ann Rodriguez

Cover designed & drawn by Gene Duplantier

INSIDE THE SAUCERS

Mr. UFOs Teenage Years

By

Timothy Green Beckley

INNER LIGHT – GLOBAL COMMUNICATIONS

INSIDE THE SAUCERS

Mr. UFOs Teenage Years!

By Timothy Green Beckley

With Additional Material By:

Allen Greenfield, Gene Steinberg, David Halperin,
Rick Hilberg, Brad Steiger, Edward J. Babcock,
Jerome Clark, Kenneth L. Larson, George D. Fawcett

Copyright © 2017 - Timothy Green Beckley DBA Inner Light/ Global Communications,
All Rights Reserved

Original Printing 1962 – Interplanetary News Service

Nonfiction - Printed in the United States of America

No part of this book may be reproduced, stored in retrieval system or transmitted in any form or by any means, electronic, mechanical, photocopying, recording, without express permission of the publisher.

Timothy Green Beckley: Editorial Director,
Carol Rodriguez: Publishers Assistant,
Proofreader and Editor: Sean Casteel
Layout: Tim R. Swartz
Editorial Assistant: William Kern

Original Cover Art By Gene Duplantier
Color Rendition: Carol Rodriguez

For free catalog write:
Global Communications
P.O. Box 753
New Brunswick, NJ 08903

Free Subscription to Conspiracy Journal E-Mail Newsletter: www.conspiracyjournal.com

Email: mrufo8@hotmail.com

Mr. UFOs Secret UFO Files – YouTube

https://www.youtube.com/user/MRUFO1100

CONTENTS

BACK A BIT IN TIME – FLYING SAUCER STYLE - By Timothy Green Beckley 7

WELL, THERE WE WERE! - By Allen Greenfield 13

FROZEN IN TIME - By Gene Steinberg 17

NOTES FROM THE PAST - By Jerome Clark 21

COMING TO BELIEVE IN FLYING SAUCERS - By David Halperin 25

FORMER TEEN UFOLOGISTS - By Rick Hilberg 27

FOREVER ALLIES - By Brad Steiger 29

FOREWORD - By Timothy Green Beckley 33

THE STATUS OF UFOLOGY TODAY - By Edward J. Babcock 37

UFOs 1962 41

FOREIGN SIGHTINGS OF 1962 - By Jerome Clark 59

COMMENT ON THE UFO MYSTERY - By Timothy Green Beckley 71

THE BENDER MYSTERY AND THE ANSWER TO THE FLYING SAUCER RIDDLE
By Timothy Green Beckley and Jerome Clark 83

THE UFO IN THE COFFER IN THE GREAT PYRAMID OF GIZA - By Kenneth L. Larson 99

A FLYING SAUCER 15-YEAR SUMMARY - By George D. Fawcett 107

BACK A BIT IN TIME – FLYING SAUCER STYLE

By Timothy Green Beckley

A lot of boys my age were probably starting to think about girls and sneaking a peek at their father's Playboy collection. Well, it took me a few years to get into the sins of the flesh. (As it turned out, about ten years later, I became the adult movie review critic for "*Hustler Magazine*.") Instead, at 14 or 15, I was reading magazines like "*Fate*" and "*Flying Saucers From Other Worlds*." And, along the way, I hooked up with a small collective of other would-be teen UFOlogists.

Let me clarify: we weren't particularly geeks or nerds (such terms hadn't even been coined yet), but we did have some fairly lofty ideals when it came to the subject of flying saucers and their presumed alien crews. Lured by the magic of NASA's earliest missions and a full-blown nationalistic battle to beat the Russians into orbiting a satellite, we were more into the cosmos than into what we possibly thought at the time were more mundane earthly matters…like keeping our grades up in school.

By "coincidence," we all met through a column in Ray Palmer's digest magazine. "*Flying Saucers*" was an offbeat, bantam-sized publication that cost a whopping thirty-five cents and which you either had to subscribe to or hunt for in the back rows and racks of some pretty obscure newsstands. Palmer had edited a pulp science fiction magazine out of Chicago called "*Amazing Stories*," where he tied in underground civilizations, lost worlds and the sightings of some pretty strange, fan-dangled, whirling disc-shaped objects that were just beginning to be seen in the sky all over the United States following World War II.

It was 1962-63 and we were thirsty for knowledge. There was no Internet. No cell phones. So, if you had an inquisitive mind, you read. And if you were into UFOs, Palmer's zine was about the only ballgame in town devoted entirely to the subject. And I know I was eager to seek out others who shared my interest and might have information to exchange. And so on my manual typewriter I wrote a letter to Palmer Publications about my interests and he published it alongside similar communiqués. Correspondence was exchanged through the mail with others who had gotten my address from the pages of this strange little magazine devoted to a very fringe topic. In fact, we were making friends all over the world, in countries that we couldn't immediately pinpoint on the map.

I suppose I think of myself as a second generation UFO researcher. Or more accurately as a Fortean mindful of the depth and scope of Charles Fort's contribution to unexplained phenomena and his dedication of hours spent going through dusty newspaper files and scientific journals gathering dust in libraries in the U.S. and the UK.

Truth is, I wasn't on the scene when the National Investigations Committee on Aerial Phenomena was formed, nor did I ever become a member of APRO, the Aerial Phenomena Research Organization, which was a bit more liberal-minded when it came to UFOs, who was inside, and what their mission in coming to earth might be. NICAP was strictly "nuts-and-bolts," as we say, and was determined to prove that UFOs were physical craft from outer space. They went after reports by pilots, cops and scientific types, while APRO was keen on collecting reports of humanoid beings seen in association with the craft. They were picking up reports from all over Europe and South America, while NICAP centered its attention on butting heads with the Air Force over what they felt was an attempt to stonewall the topic and to keep the saucers a closely guarded secret from the American public.

At some point – circa 1963/64 – I decided to throw my own saucer-shaped hat into the UFOlogical ring and start my own organization as well as an affiliated publication which we called (no drum roll necessary on this uninspired name) *"The Interplanetary News Service Report."*

The organization and its publication quickly grew from a few dozen members to over 1500, probably making us the third largest organization of its type in the country. Some members knew my age, others didn't – none seemed to care! I was putting out a pretty impressive 40 page publication with the aid of some very credible – and incredible – associates, until I got an offer from Jim Moseley which I couldn't refuse, allowing him to take over our rank and file membership roster and combine our subscriptions with his more professionally-produced magazine *"Saucer News."* To sweeten the pot, he offered to make me Managing Editor of his magazine and to pay me a weekly salary. Hell, how could I say no? I guess this sort of officially ended my career as a teenage UFOlogist, but not as a "teenage werewolf" as I went on to produce a couple of B-movie horror films under the moniker of Mr. Creepo.

I could blow by you a lengthy list of names of those who started out around the same time as I did in a quest for the truth about the "Space Brothers," but the majority has disappeared, if indeed they even stuck around long enough to be considered part of the scene.

I do remember fondly several aspiring individuals who have passed on to some heavenly realm or other dimension, but should be acknowledged as to the role they played, both in the development of my career and in UFO matters in general. There would be Al Manak of *"Flying Saucer Digest"* fame, Gray Barker, my first major book publisher and the editor of *"The Saucerian,"* and, of course, *"Saucer News"* publisher Jim Moseley, the court jester of a budding field of research who managed to keep things moving and grooving, even during the periods when the saucers weren't flying so thick and fast through our atmosphere. (Made a crank phone call when in doubt to stir up the pot and get the likes of contactee George Adamski to espouse another fanciful story, real or imagined.)

But we digress and are getting off the topic of teenage UFOlogy just a bit. In fact, those who want to pursue the beginning of my career and the smiling cherub faces of those who set up camp at around the same time are welcome to hear a recent pod cast of TheParacast.com, hosted by a graduate of those same teen years. Gene Steinberg, perhaps a year or two older, but not any wiser, was one of the original teens now turned senior – and serious – UFOlogist, like the rest of us. In any regard, we were all pretty wet behind the Martian ears in those days, and you can rest assured that it can be said that we are still floundering about looking for answers to the same questions that perplexed us in the 1960s and Seventies.

With the help of a section called "Saucer Club News" in Ray Palmer's *"Flying Saucers"* magazine in the 1950s and 1960s, enterprising young people got together to form their own UFO clubs, or just looked to meet up with others with the same interests. That's where such people as your humble host of The Paracast and such notables as Tim Beckley, Jerome Clark, Allen Greenfield and Rick Hilberg got their starts. In a single virtual room, Gene's old friends will reminisce about their early work in the UFO field. The political and cultural climate, how both may have impacted early research efforts, are also debated. Guest co-host is J. Randall Murphy.

Okay, in addition to yours truly who was busy grinding out the latest news on an old fashioned mimeograph machine (a printing device first patterned by Thomas Edison), there were others putting staples into printed sheets of 8.5x11 paper to create their own zines.

INSIDE THE SAUCERS - MR. UFOS TEENAGE YEARS

I always felt I had the best "amateur" publication around, though crude by today's standards, thanks in large part to Jerry Clark, who typed the master stencils for our issues, thus giving us a nearly perfect newsletter free of the typos and grammatical errors that would creep in when I tried to do the job myself.

Clark quickly went on to bigger and better ventures, eventually penning the monumental "**UFO Encyclopedia**" (in three huge volumes), becoming editor of *Fate* magazine, and winding up "at the side" of the late astronomer Dr J. Allen Hynek at the very prestigious Center For UFO Studies in Chicago. (Enthusiasts may do a search for Jerome Clark on my YouTube channel, "Mr. UFO's Secret Files" to hear a reflective, personal account of his adventures over the ensuing decades.)

I don't need to go into detail here regarding the others, i.e. Steinberg, Hilberg, Halperin and Greenfield since I have specifically requested they add a bit of color to this publication by outlining their humble roots, how their interests and beliefs have developed, and where we can expect to go from here (at seventy, not very far, I would assume).

And speaking of this publication, I should mention somewhere along the line – this being the first ample opportunity without backtracking and rewriting everything – that the publication you decided not to resist our highly polished pitch for – and paid your hard earned cash to obtain – is an exact duplicate of my first book that came off our mimeograph press circa 1963.

In order to defray the cost of printing our "*Interplanetary News Service Report*" (far from being covered by the $2.00 subscription fee), we needed to invent a way to keep our asses out of debt and pay the hyperbolic postage and shipping costs (out of hand even in those days before rampant inflation). We hit upon the concept of publishing some sort of book or booklets of around 70 to 100 pages. "**Inside The Saucers**" was the first project of its type. Today, my company, Inner Light – Global Communications, has around 270 titles posted on Amazon that I hope you will consider adding to your paranormal library.

As stated, we have done virtually no editing here. What you read in 1963 is what you will read here today. Sean Casteel, my editor, has maybe found a few commas out of place and an occasional typo that got past Jerry Clark's initial eagle eye and the white out process. (Remember white out? It was used to correct stencils if you found an error, but it made such a mess that you might have been better off letting the original error go through just as it was.)

Reading over the retyped manuscript, I must say I am impressed with the tone of this work. We had some original thinking going for ourselves, and I do believe I have to take credit for having come forward with the idea that some of the flying discs being observed might be of Nazi origin (see the crudely sketched facsimile of a German built saucer within these pages).

We also tore into the reputed appearance of the Men In Black (done so before my softcover book "*UFO Silencers*" hit the bestseller charts) and offered researcher Ken Larson a speculative arm to espouse his theory that there was a sort of synchronicity between UFOs, the Great Pyramid and the Salton Sea (a rather bleak and barren California wetland-like watering hole that time has forgotten – and it's no wonder why, if you care to Google photos of the Salton Sea as it exists today). There is also an inspiring section by the late George Fawcett, who at one time had the largest private collection of UFO photos, and a detailed report on saucers sightings from 1962. Perhaps the most credible case described herein involved a UFO flap at the Oradell, New Jersey Reservoir. Old timers will recall the excitement caused by UFOs that bored a hole in the ice at the Wanaquee, New Jersey Reservoir, but the incident at Oradell seems more impressive and never got any recognition. Deserves being scrutinized very carefully for its possible relevance and importance as a historical benchmark.

Anyway, as far as I am concerned, "*Inside The Saucers*" is a forgotten treasure and we can't thank Rick Hilberg enough for discovering one of the few remaining copies in his files in Cleveland and making a photocopy from which the original work was retyped most meticulously by Sean Casteel.

Timothy Green Beckley - August, 2017

Timothy Green Beckley

WELL, THERE WE WERE!

By Allen Greenfield

WELL, there we were. Every year, right before and after New Year's, I'd go to NYC and have a marathon gabfest with all the UFOlogists of note in New York and nearby Jersey: Tim Beckley, Gene Steinberg, Jim Moseley, Rabbi Yonah ibn Aharon, Jack Robinson and Mary Robinson, John Keel, Dave Halperin – all kinds of UFO "buffs" (as Keel liked to call us). Some years it got truly bizarre. There weren't any drugs or alcohol (well, maybe Jim, but the man never drew a sober breath that I knew of; drinking and chain smoking and a minor in drugs, he still lived into his eighties. Shakes your faith in good health practices, but he was an unusual guy.)

There was, however, sleep deprivation. It was the 1960s, and sometimes we ran a saucer-fest for 72 hours, pausing briefly to watch the ball drop below us in Times Square...from the hotel room of course – I only recall one year we went outside and watched "live" on the street. I also noted a bagel vendor drop his entire cartful, pick them up off of Broadway and go back to selling them. Ah, little ole New York.

One time Gene and I literally hashed out the UFO mystery for 72 hours straight. Finally, Gene's dad showed up in uniform, probably thinking his son had been abducted. I woke up once in the middle of a sentence – which is ok, except I was the one who was talking, or trance-channeling or whatever.

One year we decided to invite Stan Lee to the party. At 2 AM. Stan declined, but with good humor. I think.

Then there was the year we decided to go over to Jim Rigberg's Flying Saucer News bookstore, right through Central Park. Around 3 AM. It was a time when "West Side Story" was big on Broadway, and it turns out three of the four of us were carrying switchblades. I started snapping my fingers, and popping my knife. Soon I was joined by my companions, and we were snapping, clicking and singing "Cool, Cool" from "West Side Story."

INSIDE THE SAUCERS - MR. UFOS TEENAGE YEARS

Horrors! A lady walking a tiny poodle comes walking towards us, pretends not to notice us, but we all knew this was her worst nightmare. I turned around when she passed but she had vanished. I don't know if she and Poopsie had ducked behind a bush or – more likely – had been abducted by aliens. Fear draws them, you know. Or maybe she was an alien (or Poopsie was, and she was just a robot) checking out the UFOlogists. If so, her report explains why there hasn't been any alien invasion.

Rigberg was very nice to us, but cautioned us to avoid "the dangerous boys in the park." We said nothing.

I met Tim and Gene through Ray Palmer's free ads in *"Flying Saucers Magazine"* under *"Saucer Club News."* We all had little magazines ("zines") and some sort of club. This all wound up in the 50-year run of the Congress of Scientific UFOlogists, later called the National UFO Conference. Jim Mosely organized our biggest gathering in June 1967 at the Commodore Hotel. Thousands attended, even the "love candidate" for president; the head of the Air Force contact UFO project; James "the Amusing" Randi, just back from Peru; and the TV star Roy Thinnes from the then-current "X Files"- type show called "The Invaders." (Actually, Roy Thinnes showed up in the 1990s in "The X Files" as an alien in several episodes.) It was 1967, the Summer of Love, and it apparently made The Donald so mad he tore down the hotel and built Trump Tower.

Y'all know the rest.

It was a celestial time.

Allen Greenfield

Allen Greenfield

Allen Greenfield has been in the UFO biz almost since the beginning. He has been on the board of the National UFO Conference (NUFOC) since its inception and was there in the 1950s and '60s along with James Moseley, Gray Barker, and later, Tim Beckley as they pulled off legendary UFO conferences attended by thousands.

Greenfield is a long-time student of esoteric spirituality and Gnosticism, a study he began in 1960. A past (elected) member of the British Society for Psychical Research, the National Investigations Committee on Aerial Phenomena (NICAP) (from 1960), he has twice been the recipient of the "UFOlogist of the Year Award" of the National UFO Conference. He is a Borderland Science Research Associate (BSRA). Asa futurist with a remarkable track record of giving accurate predictions of future history, he is also a past President of the Atlanta Science Fiction Organization (ASFOII), which pioneered the prototype for science fiction conventions as they are now commonly presented.

Greenfield is the author of several books; "**Secret Cipher of the UFOnauts**" has been critically acclaimed in many reviews all over the world. Allen says that he has long believed that the mind-expanding rituals of Western Occultism may be an important key to the solution of the UFO enigma. A more scholarly work, "**The Story of the Hermetic Brotherhood of Light**" which deals with this seminal occult group from a Thelemic perspective was published in 1997. Greenfield was also a contributing author for the book "**Angel Spells: The Enochian Occult Workbook Of Charms, Seals, Talismans And Ciphers**," published by Inner Light-Global Communications.

www.bibliotecapleyades.net/cienciareal/cienciareal27a.htm

FROZEN IN TIME

By Gene Steinberg

IN 1962, I was still attending high school. An overweight kid from Brooklyn, I didn't make friends easily, and thus I sought other ways to find fellow travelers. You see, I was a flying saucer enthusiast.

It wasn't a fatal condition, but it sure set me apart from the crowd. As a result, I sort of lived apart from the world; only two nearby friends shared that interest. But, over the years, they grew up and got real lives, more or less.

So most of the people I knew well were pen pals. We discovered each other in the pages of Ray Palmer's "Flying Saucers" magazine, in a section called "Saucer Club News." We were rich, poor, middle class, with different family backgrounds and religions, but we shared an interest in those mystifying strange discs in the skies.

In that year, one of my fellow travelers, Tim Beckley, was busy establishing himself as a book publisher. One of his early works, "Inside the Saucers 1962," was, as the title implied, a compendium of sightings and speculation.

It's a document that's very much frozen in time in one respect, but it also demonstrates just how little the UFO field has changed in the ensuing 55 years. But there are some notable passages that you might want to consider in a wider perspective.

So, early on, Beckley states, "The reason no UFOs have crashed is probably that their pilots have perfect control."

These words were written 15 years after the alleged UFO crash at Roswell, but the myth mostly stayed under-the-radar until it was rediscovered in the late 1970s by Charles Berlitz, William Moore and Stanton Friedman.

Yet another passage in the book is worth attention, Beckley's conclusion that, "The climax to the saucer saga may or may not come in the near future. Only time will answer this question, but it is safe to say that it is in the foreseeable future."

I suppose that depends on how you define "foreseeable future," though we all felt optimistic then that the UFO mystery would be solved before long. Certainly Beckley had his own suspicions and expectations, as best exemplified by his use of the name "Interplanetary News Service Report" for his first magazine.

How things have changed.

But even if you look at this book as a relic of a forgotten past, it's very much a reflection of a time of optimism, in the days before we all grew jaded after the death of a young President. Its pages recount a number of compelling cases that still cry out for solutions. You'll also see evidence of the amazing maturity of the young man who assembled all of this material in a cogent, well-written format.

Just reading through the book brought back memories of days gone by, at a time when things seemed to change at a dizzying pace. So, within a year, I had lost all that extra weight - and I've kept it off. My career paths led me to writing and broadcasting, and it was all inspired by my interest in flying saucers.

I am still friends with many of the people I first met in those days of yore: Allen Greenfield, Jerome Clark, David Halperin, Rick Hilberg and, of course, Tim Beckley.

This small book is rich with possibilities, the beginnings of an amazing journey that continues through to this very day.

Have we come close to the journey's end yet? Not by a long shot!

Gene Steinberg
Host/Executive Producer, "The Paracast"
Mesa, AZ
August 17, 2017

Gene Steinberg

Gene Steinberg is an award-winning journalist who first discovered the magic of writing while still a teenager. He edited his own science fiction and New Age fanzine, and began writing a science fiction novel about an Earth man who finds himself in an unknown land faced with life-threatening situations.

Over the years, Gene also developed a strong interest in UFOs and other paranormal phenomena, and wrote and edited a number of commentaries on the subject. In fact, during the time he worked as a radio broadcaster, covering a traditional news beat, he was still out and about exploring the paranormal on the side, with the kind indulgence – or supreme tolerance – of his employers.

Today, he hosts one of the most popular broadcast and online offbeat radio shows. The Paracast (www.theparacast.com) is the gold standard of the paranormal. A new show is added every Sunday.

Gene Steinberg

NOTES FROM THE PAST

By Jerome Clark

WE all grew up, of course. No surprise there. The surprise is that some of us never left. UFOs and anomalies fell into the fabric of our lives, a continuing fascination, just as often an irritation, the levels of interest fluctuating over time, but always a presence.

I spent most of the 1990s researching and writing the multi-volume "***UFO Encyclopedia***," a summing up of decades' worth of exposure and reflection. Much of that necessitated digging through archives, some of which resulted in my reintroduction to the saucer newsletters and bulletins of the early 1960s, where often enough I encountered my by-line attached to some dated and naive contribution.

Like the teenage ufologists I connected with back in those days, I was bursting with curiosity and wonder, which could have taken me almost anywhere but which, because I'd read Edward J. Ruppelt's sober "***The Report on Unidentified Flying Objects***" a year after its 1956 publication, led me to flying saucers, then to Charles Fort, Donald E. Keyhoe, M. K. Jessup, Frank Edwards, Harold T. Wilkins, and other first-generation UFO authors. I joined NICAP. Meantime, I was engaged in correspondence – writing out my letters on a typewriter that was even then ancient, retired from the local railroad depot where my dad worked as telegrapher – with David Halperin, Timothy Green Beckley, Gene Steinberg, Allen Greenfield, and other contemporaries, most of them now gone and forgotten.

I often observe that if the first saucer book I read had been a contactee title by George Adamski, Daniel Fry, George Van Tassel, or some lesser light, even at that tender, impressionable age I would have seen UFOs as manifest nonsense. I then would have gone on to live a life unimaginably different from the one that followed. I don't know what that life would have been, though I suspect as some kind of academic (as happened to Halperin, still a friend), but if I never made any money out of it (lazy popular stereotypes about big bucks to be harvested from UFO writing notwithstanding), I got to meet many interesting people, undergo memorable experiences, and think no end of captivating thoughts.

Naturally, I never "solved" the UFO mystery. Back in 1962 we were sure that answer could come at any moment. All we hoped was that we might be some part of that. We weren't, and UFOs and their anomalous cousins only got more, not less, impenetrable. Yes, the extraterrestrial hypothesis' principal prediction – that countless earthlike extrasolar planets, arguably hosting intelligent civilizations, would be discovered one day – has been validated in recent years, though a link between that and hard-core UFO sightings remains speculative. Proposed at various levels of cleverness and sanity, theories focusing on paranormal forces remain the same.

Even so, the road we set out on all those years ago has enabled a trip none of us would have missed. I'm still in motion, and I plan to be until I can't be.

Jerome Clark

Jerome Clark

Jerome Clark got interested in UFOs in his adolescence and became active in teen ufology in the early 1960s. He went on to an extended career as ufologist and anomalist, writing for England's "*Flying Saucer Review*" over a decade and a half. His first book, "**The Unidentified**," written with Loren Coleman, was published in 1975. He was associate editor, then senior editor, of "*Fate*" from 1976 to 1989. He served on the board of the Center for UFO Studies and edited its magazine, "*International UFO Reporter*." He is author of the prize-winning, multivolume "**UFO Encyclopedia**" (1990-1998) and other books, including "**Unnatural Phenomena**" (2005) and "**Hidden Realms**" (2010). In 2008 the Society for Scientific Exploration presented him with its Dinsdale Award for his "significant contributions to the expansion of human understanding through the study of unexplained phenomena...presented from a sophisticated perspective." He lives in Minnesota, where he contributes features, reviews, and essays to "*Fortean Times*" while pursuing a variety of other interests, including history, politics, and folk-roots music.

Jerome Clark

1965 Cleveland Congress: David Halperin, Dale Rettig, Jim Moseley, Michael Mann.

COMING TO BELIEVE IN FLYING SAUCERS

By David Halperin

I became convinced of UFO reality at age 12 going on 13, upon reading Gray Barker's ***"They Knew Too Much About Flying Saucers****.*" I believed in UFOs because I believed in the Three Men in Black, and I believed in the Three Men in Black because they were a faithful reflection of what I knew to be true from within my own home. Namely, that we had a terrible secret – that my mother was not merely a "semi-invalid," as I liked to imagine her, but was slowly dying of heart disease – which we of the household were forbidden (by our own self-imposed taboo) to speak. Gray Barker, who wrote out of his own secret as a closeted gay man in 1950s West Virginia, had expressed in symbolic, necessarily distorted terms a truth of overwhelming emotional authenticity. I responded by becoming a UFOlogist.

My belief in UFOs came with sudden revelatory power. It faded some years later, slowly and gradually. There was no one morning when I woke up and knew it wasn't true, that there were no spaceships visiting our skies. I simply became absorbed with other things. I went to college, studied ancient languages, pored over the visions of Ezekiel and the relics of the ancient Jewish ecstatic mysticism based on those visions – what's called "merkavah mysticism," which has a good deal in common with the UFO abduction experience. As a professor of religious studies at the University of North Carolina, Chapel Hill, my main area of interest was religious traditions of heavenly ascensions and otherworldly journeys. Of course, this was UFOlogy in a more respectable guise.

So I've been a UFOlogist all my life. In the controversy between UFOlogists and skeptics, I think the skeptics are right about the less important issue, namely that UFOs don't exist. I believe the UFOlogists are right about the more important issue, that within the "myth and mystery" of the UFO (as Eddie Bullard calls it) there is a vital truth that demands exploration. This truth is not about space aliens but about us, as individuals, as a culture, as a species. It's about the human soul, which contains enough alienness to fill a universe.

David Halperin

Dave Halperin's ***Journal of a UFO Investigator*** was published in 2011 by Viking Press, to strong reviews. It's appeared in Spanish, Italian and German translations. *Publishers Weekly* wrote that "Halperin's gripping debut is less about aliens than alienation." Reviewer Richard Dansky commented that "Journal of a UFO Investigator is not a science fiction novel. Rather, it's a novel about what science fiction is for and about … the ability to cast real problems in an unreal context, and by doing so, get a handle on them."

Halperin taught history of Judaism, from a basic introductory course to advanced undergraduate and graduate seminars. He also taught and published extensively on Jewish mysticism and Messianism, and on the comparative study of Judaism, Christianity, and Islam.

www.davidhalperin.net

www.davidhalperin.net/wp-content/uploads/2012/08/NJAAP-Bulletin1.pdf

Sign up for my email newsletter, delivered first Tuesday each month: http://bit.ly/2asr

David Halperin

FORMER TEEN UFOLOGISTS

By Rick Hilberg

TIM'S rerelease of his 1962 book on the UFO subject certainly does bring back some fond — and not so fond – memories of literally growing up in the wonderful, and sometimes wacky, world of "flying saucers."

My start chasing these elusive platters started way back in 1958 in elementary school where after some discussion about "flying saucers" brought up by several students in one of my classes, resulted in the teacher, sensing a true learning and research opportunity, decided to have certain members of the class research the subject and then present a pro and con "debate." Me, surprisingly I took the negative side and did my research into what I initially thought would be "a piece of cake" to completely disprove. However, even though I was committed to the con side of the question, I began to privately wonder if maybe these darn things could really exist.

It was at about this same time that I first ran across a copy of Ray Palmer's iconic "*Flying Saucers*" on a local newsstand and quickly purchased a copy. There I was properly introduced to the world of "ufology" and promptly read the whole issue cover to cover. That was it - I was indeed hooked. On that Christmas break in December of 1958 several of us young "saucer enthusiasts" (thanks to Gray Barker for that term) actually got together to discuss the subject and bring our various saucer books and magazines to share and pour over - my first organized meeting.

Anyway, as I grew a few years older and started attending the meetings of the local Cleveland Ufology Project, I became more and more active, and decided to write to some of the other young enthusiasts who used Palmer's "Saucer Club News" column to tell of their own little groups and projects. That's where I first came across and got in contact with other "teen ufologists" such as Tim Beckley, Allen Greenfield, Dale Rettig, David Halperin, Bob Easley, Gene Steinberg and a host of others. Hey, some of these other guys actually put out little newsletters, mostly just a few pages done on a mimeograph machine or a spirit duplicator (those smelly purple pages like the teachers used in school for their test papers), so maybe I should try my hand at it too. The result was a six page newsletter called *UFO Magazine*, glaring typos and all done on a tiny spirit duplicator that my Dad bought for me used at a local office supply store. I was an actual publisher!

Well, now it's more than fifty years later and I'm still chasing those damned platters. Over the years many of us teen saucer hunters got together in person and developed lifelong friendships. We all attended literally hundreds of saucer meetings and conventions, and actually founded the first "serious" non-contactee convention that had a more than forty year run in venues all across the United States. Many of us are still active in the field, either publishing or blogging on the Internet, and I just published the fiftieth anniversary issue of *"Flying Saucer Digest"* (which was founded by Al Manak and Ron Pelger), which absorbed my *"UFO Magazine"* way back in 1970.

Rick Hilberg

FOREVER ALLIES

Bless all those Teen Ufologists!

They were great supporters of young Brad as he began his UFO career with ***Strangers from the Skies*** in 1966...and they remain dear friends today.

Forever Allies!

Brad Steiger

Brad Steiger

The man from SS&S

Holding a 1971 copy of his publication (no longer published) GENE DUPLANTIER sits in his work room at home. On the wall are two oil paintings he did up north, some years ago in autumn.

Gray Barker and Jim Moseley

1979 National UFO Conference in Green Bay, WI. L to R: Tim Becley, Rick Hilberg and Jim Moseley.

At center (l-r) are Timothy Green Beckley, Author of UFO Silencers and CEO of Inner Light Publications and T Allen Greenfield, author of Secret Cipher of the UFOnauts and Secret Rituals of the UFOnauts. 32nd National UFO Conference.
(Photo by J. Moseley)

FOREWORD

THIS is the first in a series of UFO booklets to be published by the Interplanetary News Service. Future booklets will deal with landings of saucers, hostility, and one researcher's many interviews with world-famous contactees.

The year 1962 will not be soon forgotten by UFO researchers. It was a year in which American astronauts and Soviet cosmonauts sighted six strange "fireflies," and a year in which X-15 pilot Joe Walker photographed six disc-shaped objects flying behind his aircraft. Personally, this editor takes delight in sticking his neck out, which is one of reasons why this is being published in the first place. Some of the stories in the following pages are almost unbelievable, but they are representative of a part of today's research into the field of Unidentified Flying Objects.

Many of you during the past year have asked us our thoughts on the Bender mystery and Bender's book "***Flying Saucers and the Three Men***." In answer to your questions, we have extended one whole chapter to cover the Bender mystery and the three men in black. Connected with this mystery is a postcard that was sent to Bill Boyer (formerly Bill Ashbay) in January of 1962, which he forwarded on to me. We printed it in the second issue of the "*Interplanetary News Service Report*," and it brought many comments from our members, who wanted more information. The letter itself, together with more information on the individual, is included in this volume.

It is quite hard to put into words the way we feel toward all those who have helped us during the past year. Of course, all of them could not be given credit here, but in particular Jerome Clark, James M. Moseley, James Kelsey, George D. Fawcett, and Gene Duplantier cannot be easily forgotten. These persons stuck with us during the many hardships and times of need.

The Interplanetary News Service was officially started on January 4, 1962. Our membership grew until we soon became one of the leading organizations on the East Coast. Our publication was the first to carry an on-the-spot account of the now-famous "Eagle Lake Case" and to print in detailed form the sightings of fireballs in the New Jersey area on the night of April 23.

Included in this volume are a number of articles written by researchers who, like you and me, are deeply interested in the UFO phenomenon and the answer to same. Take, for instance, "A Flying Saucer 15 Year Summary" by George D. Fawcett. Mr. Fawcett has been involved in UFO happenings for well over ten years now and is currently the president of the Massachusetts and Rhode Island Two-State UFO Study Group for Adults. Along with Mr. Fawcett's article, we would like to present a new face in the world of UFOlogy: that of Kenneth L. Larson of San Francisco. His article, entitled "The UFO in the Coffer in the Great Pyramid of Giza," will prove quite startling. However, we feel that it should be presented, for what it is worth, which we believe to be a great deal. You will be hearing a lot more of Mr. Larson in the coming months, as he is now completing work on a book which he hopes to have published shortly.

Censorship through human nature and Air Force orders continued throughout the year. On February 6, the Air Force announced for the fifteenth time in fifteen years that no such objects existed, providing the public with the usual answer, one that it had indeed expected. If the Air Force is withholding UFO information, it may be doing so for good reason. Many still remember the statement made by General Douglas MacArthur to the effect that the nations of the world will have to unite against an attack by people from other planets. The General expressed similar sentiments in a speech at West Point in 1962.

X15 FILMS OBJECTS, BUT PILOT WON'T COMMENT.

Perhaps the biggest shock to UFO researchers came by way of an open letter from Dr. Leon Davidson of White Plains, New York. This letter states that the flying saucers are merely the result of psychological warfare being played by the United States Central Intelligence Agency to put a fright into America's enemies. This could be the answer, but there are too many objections to it for it to be taken seriously. The UFOs have been tracked on radar and sighted by civilians as well as Air Force pilots. Surely all these people weren't being fooled.

Of the landings reported in 1962, the most important was an incident that took place in Florida toward the end of July. (Details presented elsewhere in this book.) The sighting would never have come out into the open had it not been for Bill Dunn, Jr., of Coral Gables, Florida, an INS member who investigated the case before it was finally covered up by Air Force censorship.

The world of UFOlogy is a strange one, often frightening and exasperating, but never dull. It is true that we are being watched by entities not of this Earth. But where, exactly, do they come from? Why are they here? We shall attempt to give at least a partial answer to these and other questions in the following pages.

Timothy Green Beckley, Director, Interplanetary News Service

February 10, 1963

THE STATUS OF UFOLOGY TODAY

By Edward J. Babcock

HAVE you ever wondered if it's all worth it? I have, and no doubt every serious researcher has. The endless frustration is wearing. The repeated banalities of the Air Force, printed and broadcast ad infinitum are thrown in our face every time by the uniformed. You inevitably come to the point, as I myself have, where you wonder why you ever got into this business of grinding yourself down on a project in which you can't seem to get anywhere.

There is a feeling among UFO researchers today that events are quietly building up to worldwide recognition of these objects, their behavior and their origin. Many scientists are gradually realizing that other planets besides ours are inhabited. We are all familiar with the theory expounded by M. Agrest, a Soviet physicist-mathematician, suggesting that the Baalbek Terrace in the Anti-Lebanon foothills as a possible area for the landing of extraterrestrial beings thousands or tens of thousands of years ago. Hermann Oberth, a pioneer of rocket development, believes that "the flying saucers come from other worlds." Clyde Tombaugh, discoverer of the planet Pluto, who has sighted a UFO, says, "These things, which appear to be directed, are unlike any phenomenon I have ever observed. Other stars in our galaxy may have hundreds of thousands of inhabitable worlds. Races in these worlds may have been able to utilize the tremendous amounts of power required to bridge the space between the stars." Professor C.F. Powell, Dean of the Faculty at Brustik University, has said, "We may very reasonably suspect that there are beings within our galaxy of planets with physical conditions similar to ours who have achieved a far higher form of technical development with whom I hope we will attempt to make contact."

It is a well-established fact that every major world government has stacks of UFO reports documented by Air Force pilots, astronomers, aircraft technicians, etc. The Mexican, Swedish, and Brazilian governments have admitted the existence of objects which cannot be identified with any known aircraft on Earth and have opened their files, including photographs which were proven to be real BEYOND ANY DOUBT, to the public. If these three nations confirm the existence of these objects, why is our own government so stubborn in releasing the information it has gathered over the 15-year period? Why is it holding out when other governments have expressed their opinions and released the information they have gathered?

In letters to Senators Clifford P. Case and Harrison A. Williams, Jr., and Representatives James C. Auchinclose, William T. Cahill, George M. Wallhauser, Hugh J. Addonizio, and Dominick V. Daniels, of New Jersey, Colonel George M. Lockhart of the Congressional Inquiry Division, said in March, 1962, "There is no truth to the allegations that the Air Force withholds or otherwise censors information vital to public understanding or evaluation of the nature of UFOs." Every segment of that statement is totally false! Air Force censorship is proven by the following points:

a.) Air Force regulation 200-2, which orders all Air Force personnel not to discuss UFOs with "unauthorized persons unless so directed and then only on a need-to-know basis."

b.) Major Dewey Fournet, USAF-R, former Intelligence Monitor of the UFO Investigative Agency, Project Blue Book: "The Air Force has withheld and is still withholding UFO information, including sightings reports."

c.) Captain Edward J. Ruppelt, former Blue Book chief: "I was continually told, 'Tell them about the cases we've solved. Don't mention the unknowns.'"

d.) Withholding of UFO information has been confirmed by House Speaker John W. McCormack and Rep. Joseph E. Karth of the House Science and Aeronautics Committee. It has been confirmed by Senators Byrd, Goldwater, Hart, Javitz, Kefauver, Kuchel, Keating, Caso, Williams, Long and Representatives Baumhart, Holmes, Schorer, Auchincloss, Daniels and Milliken.

In mid-1959, the Adjutant General of the Army, Major General R.V. Lee, implied that it is the duty of the military services to thwart our attempts to give UFO information to the American people.

This frank admission of the military's intention to control public thinking was made in an official letter to Rep. Thomas N. Dowing, Virginia. "The military services would be remiss in their duty to the American public if we, by our assistance, encouraged these organizations in their sensational claims and contentions."

Even the U.S. Navy is getting into the act. In 1961, the Navy issued a document to all U.S. ships titled "OPNAV-94-P-3B" showing two sketches of UFOs, and instructions were given for rushing emergency sightings reports. This system is called MERINT, and is set up under JANAP-146, by the Joint Chiefs of Staff. With the illustration of these two UFO types specifically authorized by the Secretary of the Navy, it appears that the U.S. Navy recognizes the existence of UFOs, regardless of public Air Force denials.

The Armed Forces are clamping a tighter lid than ever on what they know about UFOs. They're deathly afraid of panic in the streets. They remember the coast-to-coast hysteria back in 1938 when the people panicked just from listening to a radio broadcast by Orson Welles about an imaginary invasion of Earth by men from Mars.

They're afraid of what would happen if Joe Blow and his wife, who lost their balance over something imaginary, were informed from official sources that flying saucers are real things beyond Earth's present technology.

Inquiries about the so-called flying saucers in official circles in Washington lead to a blank wall that daily grows thicker and higher. All sightings are now under tight security controls. All reports are officially censored. People who report sightings are laughed at officially, but behind the scenes the Air Force is checking on every sighting. What is the motive of the Air Force in issuing conflicting statements on UFOs?

In conclusion I can say that:

1. Reliable reports from airline pilots, airport traffic control workers, radar experts and other trained observers indicate there are intelligently controlled objects flying around the Earth, both in and outside our atmosphere, at fantastic speeds, defying Newton's Law of Gravity, in that they are not subject to inertia or metal stress.

2. These objects seem to have a relationship to a wide variety of other aerial phenomena, including earthquakes, sky-quakes, mysterious lights, angel hair, fireballs and a great many others. These also include strange movements on the moon and other planets.

3. Such objects represent at least 10% of all the objects seen in the sky.

4. They probably come from another solar system or the fourth dimension.

5. They are undoubtedly on expeditions of exploration as is evidenced by many UFO reports during the past few years.

6. The reason no UFOs have crashed is probably that their pilots have perfect control.

7. This is the most important unsolved mystery in the world today.

You know, all this secrecy scares me! It makes me think there might be some great danger facing us, and I wonder if my three years of investigation haven't misled me, for I am of the opinion that the UFOs, though their existence is beyond all doubt, are not a menace to us. I have a feeling that behind all this veil of secrecy is nothing but an admission that the body in charge, the Pentagon, knows less than perhaps we do about what the flying saucers really are.

Is the government hiding UFO facts? Yes! But it certainly is the poorest job of secrecy on record!

UFOs 1962

TO say that the year 1962 started out with a bang would be an understatement. On January 3 came a UFO report from Woonsocket, Rhode Island. Joseph Ferriere of the Fairmount Dye Works, Willis Harnois and Rene Fauthier reported watching three circular, silver-colored discs maneuvering for from five to seven minutes. The objects, they said, moved northeast in formation at tremendous speed. The phenomena were shiny and flat and brilliantly luminous; they hovered from 9:15 A.M. for a period of time before disappearing into the distance.

Also on the 3rd, fireballs caused residents to panic in Columbus, Ohio. It was a clear evening, when suddenly there was a spectacular burst of bluish-green light in the northwest skies. It caused the area residents to flood switchboards at police and radio stations, and even WBNS-TV received calls. The calls began coming in at 6:30 P.M. and continued until after nine. There were reports that the UFO had landed in Columbus, but this went unconfirmed.

It was also sighted over Dayton, Lima, Cincinnati, and Fort Wayne, Indiana. Jets were scrambled from Dayton Air Force Base to investigate the UFO. A Cincinnati woman said she saw it come close to the ground and then rise again. A North High School sophomore in Columbus stated that he was watching through a 152-power telescope and was able to see a cabin with red and white flashing lights coming from within. He also said he could see windows in the saucer.

Robert Miller, then-director of the UFO Reporting Center in Newark, got the following statement from Philip Bougher, the observer: "I first saw the UFO about 9:15 P.M. when it was pointed out to me by my mother. I immediately went for my telescope. It is a 2.5 reflector. Being an amateur astronomer, I could tell at once that it was not a meteor. After some movement, it became stationary and changed color. I focused in on it with a 6mm eyepiece giving a power of about 150x. As I brought the object into focus, the first thing I noticed was a row of windows. THEY WERE CLEAR AND UNMISTAKABLE. Behind the windows were four lights; other than that I could not see any other details inside the windows. The object moved several times both horizontally and vertically.

"As a guess," Bougher went on, "I would say the object was approximately one-half to three-quarters of a mile away from me. I lost sight of the object when I attempted to move my telescope to another window. At times I could see something like electrical impulses. They appeared to come just before the object above and vertically to the hull. The lights inside the windows were yellow and rather soft. They were not the source of the object's brilliance. I caught sight of what I think was a sort of bluish light. As for the overall shape of the UFO, it is hard to say since I did not see the entire object at one time. I would say it was either bell-shaped of cigar-shaped." The official Air Force statement was that the object was merely a meteor. Apparently, the Air Force is somewhat more knowledgeable about meteors than even astronomers, in that it claims they can land and take off again.

In the early part of January, the West Coast and California in particular had a UFO flap with many important sightings. On January 4th Mr. and Mrs. Beryl Rawles of Ukia, California, said that on their way home about 2:30 P.M. they saw two cigar-shaped objects flying over their car in a southeasterly direction and then veering sharply to the south and disappearing over a ridge. The couple told interviewers that the machines were about thirty feet long, thirteen feet in diameter, tapering in to about six feet at either end. They also said that the objects passed within fifty feet of the car. The odd thing, Mr. Rawles said, was that no sound came from the UFOs, nor was there any sign of a vapor trail. Rawles said they were white with red trim and flew very low just above the trees. They seemed to be under perfect control at all times.

On the 5th, another unidentified flying object was sighted over Ukia. This time the UFO was coming from the southeast and flying in a northeasterly direction. One observer, Ed Giffor, said he saw a box-like UFO just below the horizon at about 4 P.M. The object, he stated, was about two-foot square and four feet long. This and the report described in the preceding paragraph were investigated and reported on by the Washington State NICAP Subcommittee.

Two days later, on January 7, at 8:00 P.M., two policemen observed an unidentified flying object as it swept through the skies over Auburn, California. Seeing the object through binoculars, Officer James Stokes reported that he observed six rays of light apparently given off by the object. The policemen sighted the object after Mr. and Mrs. Harry Joson reported having spotted it and called the Sheriff's office. Officials at Mathor Air Force Base refused to reveal just how many UFOs had been sighted.

West Coast saw "flap" during early January.

On January 15, the Los Angeles Herald Examiner, on its feature page, presented George Todt's views on the subject of unidentified flying objects. Mr. Todt described his own personal experience during the War. He had this to say about his sighting: "On one occasion a party of four of us – including a lieutenant colonel – watched a pulsating red fireball sail up silently to a point directly over the American-German front lines in 1944 during the battle of Normandy. It stopped completely for fifteen minutes before moving on."

The *El Paso Herald Post* printed the following report on January 16:

MYSTERY LIGHTS SEEN OVER CRUCES – Las Cruces, January 16.

For the third time in a year, "mystery lights" have been seen over Las Cruces. Officer Dan Garcia of the Las Cruces Police Department reported seeing s "red flash" about 5:25 A.M. yesterday morning, moving in the direction of the Organ Mountains. Later in the morning, before it became light, he saw a white light in the sky, which was not moving when he first sighted it, but "circled around" a few minutes later and disappeared. The police department said similar lights in the sky were also observed further north of the city. The radio at White Sands Missile Range told police that an aircraft over Las Cruces en route to El Paso "was just missed" by a falling star. The base is checking the incident for further reports.

On Friday, January 19, witnesses in North Carolina reported seeing a ball of fire in the sky and thought it was an airplane explosion. However, the FAA in Virginia and North Carolina said they had no aircraft missing in that area. Police Chief Howard Summers investigated reports of a UFO sighted over Mount Airy at 11:15 A.M. by at least a dozen persons. Witnesses, who saw the object for five minutes, described it as being large and round. The object was also noted to be extremely bright.

January 20 brought sightings of a hovering, orange-colored, cigar-shaped object over Woburn, Massachusetts, at 5 A.M. Jets chased it over Boston at 12:30 P.M.

On January 28, near Park Rapids, Minnesota, at Eagle Lake, a 71-year-old man named Charles Jude was tumbled out of bed by a hissing noise followed by "a kind of muffled detonation" and a terrific concussion. The next morning he noticed a peculiar cone-shaped halo in the ice. There had been a light snow, and he could find no tracks around this halo. The walls of the halo were described as being very smooth.

Mr. Jude notified Sheriff R.J. Potter, who, with a deputy, Frank Town, made an investigation. They were informed that Park Rapids is north of the Minnesota-Fargo, North Dakota, bomber run. About a week later, three professional skin divers searched for the object but said that silt made it impossible to see.

In the *Minneapolis Star* for February 19, 1962, Sheriff Potter is quoted as being "more confident than ever" that something would be found on the lake bottom. This belief, he said, was based on "something we've found."

Thinking there might be some connection between this incident and UFO activity in the area, Interplanetary News Service Assistant Editor and Minnesota District Representative Jerome Clark wrote to Sheriff Potter and inquired about new developments in the case. (This was in early April.) The Sheriff replied that nothing more had been done, as he was waiting for the ice to thaw, although anyone could look for the object as long as he informed him.

Another letter was sent to the Sheriff in mid-May. However, no reply was received.

A few weeks after the letter was sent to Mr. Potter, our Assistant Editor found that a resident of Canby, Minnesota (Mr. Clark's hometown), while driving in the Park Rapids area on January 28, late at night saw a huge ball of fire, so brilliant that it lit up the whole sky, fall to Earth near Eagle Lake. HE STATED HE WAS CERTAIN THE OBJECT WAS NOT A METEORITE.

February could certainly be called a dead month when it came to the sightings of flying saucers. To say the least, reports were few and far between.

Perhaps the two best sightings came from Canada. At approximately 10 P.M., Mrs. R. Luman phoned the Ottawa Flying Saucer Club to say that she could see a strange large object in the northeast which was giving off colored light quite discernible to the naked eye. Mrs. Luman and her daughter watched the object through binoculars for more than fifteen minutes. The object, they agreed, was circular with a bright light at the top. The remainder of this solid-looking circle gave off a red, green and bluish light. The colors seemed to shimmer.

Just about two hours later, an orange-colored UFO, round in shape, was seen by Arnold Beaton of Iroquois Falls. He stated that he came home from work at 12 midnight only to see a bright light near the back of his home. He told CIRAP investigators, "I thought the garage was on fire, but when I investigated I found instead a huge round ball over the garage." Beaton called his wife and a nearby neighbor out, and they, too, saw the object. After about five minutes, the object slowly moved away to the north.

In the first moments of dawn on February 20, astronaut John Glenn saw a fantastic sight, one that will do down in history. He spotted yellowish-green particles which he called "fireflies." The phenomena stretched out as far as he could see in either direction. Glenn discounted theories that what he had seen were snowflakes or water vapor from the jet nozzle, or even tiny copper needles from a former Air Force project.

In a book entitled "***Inside the Space Ships***," published in 1955, George Adamski, world famous contactee, told what he saw allegedly while in space aboard a Venusian spaceship. "I was amazed to see that the background of space is totally dark. Yet there were manifestations taking place all around us, as though billions upon billions of fireflies were flickering everywhere, moving in all directions, as fireflies do. However, those were of many colors, a gigantic fireworks display that was beautiful to the point of being awesome."

On the 23rd of February, a strange moving light was seen over King's Peak in Shelter Cove, California. The Eureka California Humboldt Times carried the following account:

"Anthony Machi, part owner of the Shelter Cove resort, reported last night that he saw a bright white light moving at a 'terrific rate of speed' over the King's Peak northwest of here. He said it was the fourth time he had seen the light. He said he observed it three days in a row – January 21, 22 and 23, but that it didn't shine again until last night, a clear night. He said the light moved up and down and back and forth, over both the ocean and uninhabited King's Peak. He timed it at 7:20 P.M. There have been other witnesses to the phenomenon, he said."

UFO sightings once again picked up in March, with many local papers printing reports. On the 2nd of the month, the Oregon Mail Tribune stated that mysterious objects were reported over the Trail Creek area. One observer, Carroll Watson of Shady Cove, told reporters from local UFO groups that she had been compiling reports on unidentified flying objects in the area since 1950.

An unidentified object in the sky, described as a brilliant flash and as a fiery red ball, was reported in the Berkeley California Gazette for March 10. On the same date, the Richmond California Independent printed and reviewed the story of two UFOs, both of them fiery red balls.

On the 12th of the month, George Todt's column in the *Los Angeles Herald* Examiner returned to the subject of flying saucers for the second time in just over two months. The column was entitled, "Two Kinds of Saucers?" and dealt mainly with the author's appearance on KNX radio in Hollywood and the discussion he had had with Art Wittum and Bob Sutton on the subject of UFOs.

From a news clipping sent to me by NICAP, on March 29 Charles Powers of Cumberland, Maryland, observed a bluish-silver disc-shaped object which appeared in the south, dipped down, then straight up, finally disappearing in the west. Its speed was reported to be very fast, with the sighting lasting for three or four seconds. The weather was clear, and no sound was heard.

INSIDE THE SAUCERS - MR. UFOS TEENAGE YEARS

On April 10, this editor sighted his first and only UFO. It was about 9:20 in the evening when, through a window in the west side of the house, I noticed a strange orange-colored object about the size of as a pinhead. I ran and got a pair of 7x35 binoculars which were in another room. Returning to the same window, I saw the object was fading in the northwest. At just about this time, an airplane came into view from the east, but soon vanished into the west. The object remained in view for about four minutes, and was at a height of about two miles, speeding away at a rather fast rate. It blinked every eight seconds. The wind velocity at that time was ten miles per hour and the direction was from the west. The exact temperature at the time was 59 degrees with 32 percent humidity. Upon mentioning this sighting to Alan Katz of Middlesex, New Jersey, I received the following reply:

"You mentioned as sighting you made which interests me, as it is around the time I saw my first saucer, although you gave me no details of your sighting or the date which you made it. On the 28th of April, I saw a large red flashing object with a steady white light on the bottom. The brightness increased as it moved in an erratic path. It wasn't unusually fast, but a few maneuvers it made puzzled me. I sort of shrugged it off as an optical illusion of some kind (although I should have known better), until one of my classmates told me that he and his father had seen a strange object. We described our sightings to each other, and they jibed perfectly (direction, color, speed, etc.). He had watched it through binoculars and said that it was revolving. On the 23rd this same friend, another friend, and I were in my backyard with a set of binoculars and two telescopes when we saw a fireball. It couldn't have landed more than a few blocks away, in a wooded section. This was most likely a meteor, but you should have seen it. I was facing the opposite direction when I saw a flash. This was a clear night, and it seemed odd that it was lightning. One of my friends shouted for me to look around, and I saw the fireball for a few seconds. I would rather you not put this account in the *INS Bulletin*."

And that was only the beginning of a very strange series of UFO-fireball sightings. Reports began coming into this office a few days later. We learned that also on the 23rd at 8:05 P.M. an extremely brilliant fireball passed over many parts of New Jersey with a general motion towards the west. The UFO, most observers agreed, was brighter than a full moon. The object was whitish-blue in color and followed by a short, stubby tail.

At Princeton, New Jersey, Charles H. Giffen stated that he was attracted by a great flash of light in the sky. The light threw stronger shadows than that of a full moon.

On April 19, a brilliant object flashed across the western skies about 8:15 P.M. Federal Aviation officials said, "The thing touched off alarm in Utah, Idaho, Arizona and other sections of the West." Residents of Eureka, Utah, were convinced the object, whatever it was, crashed to the Earth. They sighted a "blue flash" and a rumbling was heard in the distance. The *Salt Lake Tribune* was swamped with calls from citizens inquiring about or reporting the object. Those who saw it said it flashed across the night sky from east to west and was visible from two to four seconds. Pilots from as far east as Goodland, Kansas, and in Utah, Nevada and Arizona spotted the flash. The light was so brilliant that it caused the street lamps in downtown Eureka to go off momentarily. The fireball seemed to move west over the Pacific towards a spot some 30 miles off San Francisco, the report said. The Salt Lake Air Route Traffic Control Center stated it receive several reports indicating the object had landed. Reports of the sighting came from as far north as northern Montana and from such points as Los Angeles, the Mexican border and eastern Oregon.

On April 30, a saucer-shaped object over New Mexico was seen by three persons who watched it through a telescope. The observers were Macario Lopez, Robert L. Dobbins, and Mr. G.G. Thompson, the superintendent of schools in Magdalena.

An unidentified flying object which Ohio State University said was probably a meteor was sighted over Newark, Ohio, on the night of May 3. It was also observed in Dayton, Columbus, Cincinnati, Portsmouth and in northern Kentucky. The object was green and white, with greenish-bluish overtones.

On the 8th, John L. Black and Ron Denault sighted at 8:40 P.M. a UFO traveling at a fast clip about 15 or 20 degrees above the horizon. It made no sound and no detail was seen – only a white light. The object, whatever it was, stayed in view for five to ten minutes, until it disappeared. The UFO was completely silent.

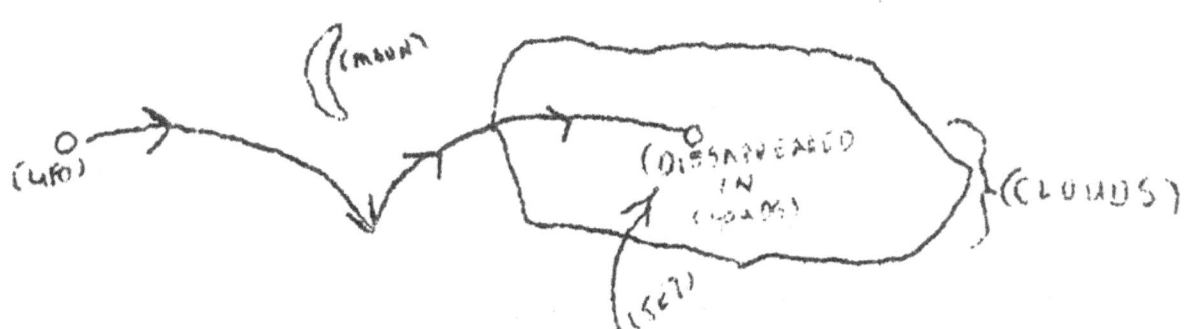

George D. Fawcett, on May 15, informed us that on the 12th at 10:30 A.M., Boston patent lawyer Robert K. Randall reported four similar objects, looking like aluminum-colored, round-topped circular saucers, moving slowly north near a transport plane that was leaving Ranscom Air Force Base.

On the following night, in the Mansfield, Ohio, area, a mysterious burning object that exploded into two distinct pieces early in the morning was followed, that evening, by many reports of a similar object, indicating, possibly, that the phenomenon was still existent. On May 23, a switchboard operator and a college teacher reported a circular "hula hoop" object having green and red lights and a yellow band around the outer edge. It was flying towards Worchester, Massachusetts.

The next day astronaut M. Scott Carpenter spotted strange space fireflies zipping past his space capsule. Previously they had been seen reported by Russian Gherman Titov and American John H. Glenn, Jr. It was rumored at the time that the fireflies were only a code name for flying saucers.

June, although nearly a dead month, did have its high points. The first day of the month brought sightings from Trenton, Bordentown and Hamilton Township, New Jersey. The Air Force said it would check into the matter to determine just what was going on. One witness stated that he thought the Air Force's viewpoint was that the UFOs were Russian satellites sent up in secret.

On July 3, the Randolph Bell family had quite an interesting time watching strange objects in the sky. Mr. Bell, his wife, two children and his half-brother, Hesse Wilson, were sitting in the yard when they saw an object like a large bright star. Three smaller objects came behind. About five minutes later the bright star moved to the east and the other three went west. About 15 minutes later, another bright object moved from north to south. The group continued to watch the objects and at 12:30 A.M. observed another UFO near the Big Dipper. Mrs. Bell stated to the American Republic that they could see jets flying but the other objects were not jets.

At 1 A.M., the morning of the 25th, half a mile south of Hackettstown, New Jersey, on the Whitehouse property, three adults saw a strange object in the sky. Raymond LaVigne, of Hackettstown, a real estate broker and former Air Force jet pilot, and his wife, Ann, were saying goodbye to Sigmund Sameth, also a real estate broker. It was a brilliantly starry night, with no moon. Their attention was first caught by four shooting stars in the west and in the south. They then spotted an object that was radiating waves of the same color. At first, Mr. Sameth thought these rays were caused by faulty vision, but he then squinted, bringing no change. The three then compared their descriptions, which were identical, even to the forked ray on the lower right hand corner. They all agreed that the object, from ray to ray, was near the size of the full moon; however, Mr. LaVigne thought that the rays were not rays at all but rings similar to the rings of Saturn. He said the rings at 12 o'clock curved down to 1 o'clock. It was agreed that the object itself, which was circular, was about five times larger and brighter Polaris, and also that through the area of the rays or rings there was a luminous area similar to the aurora of the sun seen through a mist.

The group observed the object for about five minutes. Then Mr. Sameth left and the LaVignes watched for about ten minutes before retiring. In all this time, the object did not move. Mr. LaVigne said he was sure it was not a UFO.

However, James S. Pickering, Assistant Astronomer of the American Museum, Hayden Planetarium, wrote, "I am sorry that I did not recognize it as any astronomical body, and since I was not fortunate enough to see it, I cannot even hazard a guess as to what it may have been."

In the Everglades National Park, towards the end of July, three saucers were discovered taking a sunbath in a clearing. The witnesses to this sighting three park rangers and six visitors. The incident took place near ranger headquarters in Flamingo, Florida, at midday.

The saucers, which remained for three to four minutes, were 18 feet in diameter and six feet in depth. The one ranger who stayed for the longest period of time said the machines lifted slowly off the ground and then sped up in a vertical motion until they were out of sight. As they left the ground, they reportedly let out a loud roar, with a seemingly shrill sound almost like that of a whistle. The UFOs had no smoke or exhaust fumes, but the next day, when a Geiger counter was brought in, it indicated a high level of radiation.

It is quite interesting to note that, after this report was published in a number of magazines, we received the following letter from NICAP's Richard Hall, from which we quote, in part:

"Dear Mr. Beckley:

"In the October issue of '*Saucers, Space & Science*,' we read the account of the reported landing of three UFOs in the Everglades near the end of July. Your '*Interplanetary News Service*' is cited as the source.

"Since this is a potentially very important case, which we would like to follow up on, investigate and document, could you please send us a photocopy (or loan us the original copy, which we will return) of the newspaper clipping or other original source of your information? If we are able to complete an investigation, you will be notified of the results."

This letter was dated and stamped October 3, 1962. We gladly sent all the information we had, including the original copy of the letter (a personal one to this researcher) stating that we would like to have it returned. To this date, we have heard nothing. Frankly, we are beginning to wonder just what NICAP does with all this information!

An AP release from Portland, Oregon, on July 31 stated that two fast-moving objects were seen just ahead of our American satellite Echo One. A Portland television station was jammed with calls from its viewers, who wanted to know what the object was. No answer was given.

In Pasadena, California, a biologist working on an experiment to detect life on Mars questioned theory that life exists throughout the universe. In an AP release during early August, Dr. Norman H. Horowitz of the California Institute of Technology, working on a National Aeronautics and Space Administration project, said that many people believe there's life on millions of planets. "This is an exciting and aesthetically pleasing idea," he said. "But it seems more reasonable that the origin of life was a highly important event. I believe that a realistic assessment of the problem would show that the spontaneous generation of the self-replicating molecule such as we suppose the first living thing to have been is exceedingly improbable in a random universe."

The following is a report carried by the *New York World-Telegram & Sun*:

"Edwards Air Force Base, California – UPI – August 9

"A possibility the X-15 encountered strange phenomena in space arose today with scientists unable to identify a mysterious object both sighted and photographed by Maj. Bob White on a soaring flight by the rocket ship.

"Scientists said yesterday they could not explain the objects that appeared near the X-15 on July 17 when White skyrocketed to nearly 60 miles.

"Space agency scientists said, 'We aren't even sure that what White saw and the camera photographed were two different objects.' The National Aeronautics and Space Administration, after studying White's sighting report and films from a tail movie camera on the X-15, released photographs of an object that darted above and behind the plane.

"The film reveals an object that looks like a fluttering piece of paper and which scientists described as being gray-white.

"White, from his cockpit near the nose of the rocket ship, has reported seeing what looked to him like a piece of paper the size of his hand going along with the ship at an altitude of 270,000 feet – over 50 miles high.

"The movie films captured shots of an object flitting past the roar of the supersonic craft on the same flight and at the same altitude.

"'The object – or objects – were of undetermined size,' scientists said, 'because we don't know the distance they were from the ship to make such a comparison.'"

This sighting was best covered in an article by Rev. Guy J. Cyr that was published in *"The Cosmic Researcher,"* the official publication of the Correspondence Organization for the Research of Aerial Phenomena.

At 10 P.M. the night of August 11, from Legion Field in Hackettstown, New Jersey, Steve Ozyjowski, his son Steve Jr., (15), both of Great Meadows, and Wendy Raffalco, (11), of Irvington, were watching a fireworks display to the east when they observed an object in the north that appeared to be a normal star, except that it had a bluish tint. It moved for about five seconds in a west-east direction, leaving a straight purple trail. During this time it covered a distance of comparable to five inches on a ruler held at arm's length. The UFO then disappeared.

In the early evening of Tuesday, August 21, John D. Billows and his two daughters (9 and 10), of Great Meadows, New Jersey, were driving home on the Hope Road when they observed to the west a silvery object at about 45 degrees in the sky. It looked metallic and circular, about the size of a penny, and was viewed for over ten minutes.

Perhaps just as mysterious as the Eagle Lake case (referred to earlier) is the search for a long metal object which was seen to fall into Twin Lake near Concord, South Carolina, on August 29. Divers were called to the scene, but they failed to find any object. This report was carried in the Daily Home News the following day.

On September 5 two Trans-Canada Airlines pilots flying some 80 miles apart reported that strange objects, believed to be burnt-up parts of Russian satellite Sputnik IV, seemed to appear between their two aircraft. A Vilas, Wisconsin, county deputy said he and several fellow officers spotted approximately 24 unidentified objects streaking from west to east shortly before dawn. That same evening, on the Huntley-Brinkley News (NBC-TV), the report was given, stating that the objects strung together in a closely-knit line.

Three days later an 18-inch long object was found on a country road near Seattle, Washington. An Air Force spokesman stated that they had no idea as to its significance nor its source. The sighting, which was carried by the AP wire service, reached most local and national newspapers.

Perhaps the most remembered sightings for us New Jersey residents took place during the entire month of September. They began when three boys told police they had seen a strange oval-shaped craft land in the Oradell Reservoir on Saturday, September 15, at 7:55 P.M. The trio said the object hovered over the water, submerged for a few seconds, and then rose vertically and disappeared. To back up this story, a fisherman on the opposite side of the Reservoir reported hearing a large splash at just about the time the boys said the object hit the water.

The following day two Emerson youths reported once again to the police that they sighted a strange object, similar to the one reported the day before, dip behind some trees bordering the Reservoir. A few seconds later, they reported a noise like a car door slamming but to them it sounded much louder. The boys described the saucer as being domed and having two portholes along its perimeter. At this time, the parents of the witnesses were called by local police and warned that their sons were to refrain from speaking about the matter since the government had requested a secrecy policy.

Just two days later over 120 persons flocked to the Reservoir in hopes of seeing the returning UFO. Many brought along binoculars and cameras in order to observe and record the craft. On the same night, some six hours later, two Westwood policemen reported a fast-moving cone-shaped object, while still others saw strange beams of light and strange fast-flying red discs.

The panic broke out again the following day, Wednesday, September 19, when heavy rain dampened the spirits of many. Still, some 20 persons turned out at the Reservoir in hopes of seeing a spaceship from another world. However, nothing turned up that day except stories of strange tracks in the nearby woods and 14-foot men carrying what was taken to be a shotgun.

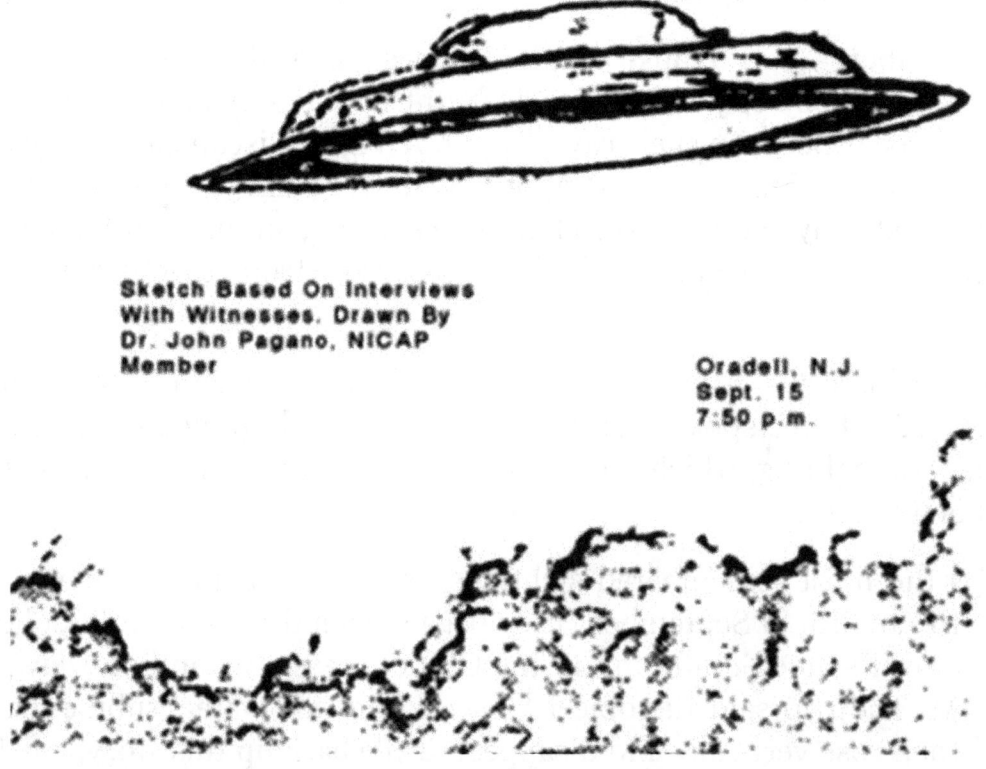

Sketch Based On Interviews With Witnesses. Drawn By Dr. John Pagano, NICAP Member

Oradell, N.J.
Sept. 15
7:50 p.m.

By this time, everyone was getting into the act, including four Emerson boys, who spotted a saucer-shaped object similar to, but different from, the above objects, near the Reservoir. They told police that three jet fighters approached the UFO but disappeared under it.

As a vivid and fitting close to an exciting week, two formations of six large bright white objects were seen. They were spotted over Pulaski Park in Hackensack by some youngsters and their parents, while over 200 persons atop Garret Mountain in East Paterson played host to a similar display.

Despite these sightings, the Hackensack Record the following week published a letter from a group of Fergenfield boys who claimed they had constructed and flown this craft themselves. The object, they stated, was nothing more than a helium balloon with a balsawood frame, said to be controlled by radio.

However, the following evening, nine persons, including five Hawthorne police officers, reported that they spotted a multicolored light in the sky over the Sam Braon quarry in Hawthorne at 4:08 A.M.

George Della Penta of Lodi, head of an independent news agency, said he and the rest of the group gathered at the quarry late Friday night and early Saturday. The purpose of this group was to see exactly what was going on in this area.

With Della Penta were Paul Paulino, a photographer, patrolman Jednoy, Welsh and Charles Kenyon, Steven Tatoki and Charles Maybey. Also present were Justin Colaarci, a guard at the quarry, and Russell Deitz, of the Passaic County Mounted Deputy Sheriffs.

At 4:08, Della Penta said, the red light came into the sky out of the northeast. He said the object, very distinctly seen through binoculars, was about 30 feet in length, about 1,000 feet in the air, and approximately two miles away.

The object changed colors from red to silver to green and back to red again. This transformation took about one minute, he said. It traveled at 100 miles an hour and stopped nearly above the witnesses. Thousands of small red particles suddenly appeared, shot toward the red glowing object and seemed to be absorbed by it. It remained above the group for about 20 minutes and then moved out of the sky towards the northwest.

Mr. Della Penta's photographer shot about 18 feet of color motion picture film and he stated that he would return to the same site later in the day to attempt once again to take photos of the object. Said Della Penta: "I didn't believe the stories about the object when I first heard about them. It is still difficult to believe. I can't figure it out."

The following night the object appeared over the same spot, seen this time by Hawthorne patrolman William Wassel. It came from the northeast, hovered in the area for 15 minutes, then disappeared in a northwesterly direction.

Once Della Penta returned with a photographer, Peter Paulino, to the top of the 550 foot cliff of the Hamburg Turnpike in Wayne. This time, though, nothing unusual was sighted.

From the above data it is quite clear that the object or objects sighted were not, indeed, helium balloons with balsa wood frames. Instead, it is more probable that they were objects which cannot be explained so easily. We must, of course, take into account the fact that many different UFOs were observed at quite a few different locations. An interesting question is how a helium balloon could dip into a reservoir and emerge again. In my mind, this is most unlikely.

Secondly, color photos of the object showing strange red particles appearing and shooting towards the UFO were taken. These particles are of particular interest to me. Could they be cosmic rays of sort, drawn in by the object for power? Of course, under normal conditions, these rays would not be visible to the naked eye, but we are dealing with a subject where little is known. Perhaps the color of the craft itself made the rays (if that is what they were) visible.

Another thing that must be taken into account is the report of the 14-foot men carrying objects that looked like shotguns. By the time so many reports had been publicized, many persons wanted to invent the wildest story possible, and this is probably how the yarn came into being. Of course, such creatures COULD have existed, but, if they did, they certainly didn't come from the Oradell saucers, as they were much too small.

Elsewhere, another report from Illinois in the last few days of September stated that police were alerted to sightings of strange UFOs being observed by early-rising residents. Upon investigation, it was found that the phenomenon was merely a 22-foot balloon launched by a group of local teenagers.

Earlier that month, on September 12, two persons about two and a half miles apart saw a white oval-shaped object, sharply outlined, about 5000 to 7000 feet in altitude. The thing made a 90 degree turn, which both witnesses saw. They are positive it was not a meteor, airplane or any other mundane phenomenon. This occurred about 9 P.M. that night.

October, although not packed with UFO sightings, did bring out the finest reported in a few months except for perhaps those in the New Jersey area. On the third, an unidentified flying object as sighted over Larson Air Force Base near Moses Lake,

Washington. The county sheriff quoted an unknown observer as saying a tear-shaped object with a red bottom and blue top was reported over the base by a security guard.

On October 12, great gobs of white sticky material fell from the sky above the Utah Power and Light Company, settling in balls and sheets as well as threads. Some pieces were 60 to 70 feet long and gave the appearance of a tattered parachute. But the substance was sticky, and it disintegrated into nothing when stretched too far.

Peter Beloz, a transmission engineer, said, "At first it looked like two or three parachutes coming down. Then as it came closer, we saw it was big globs of this stuff. A lot of it got tangled up in the transmission lines, but it didn't cause any trouble. It was all over the place. I've never seen anything like it before."

He said some of it was in big balls, while other parts were in sheets and threads. "It looked like a tarantula spider web," he said. The material came from the north and fell from the sky for 15 or 20 minutes, apparently mostly in the area of the Gadsby plant.

No one knew what the mysterious substance was, but guesses ranged from something caused by the Hercules explosion Wednesday afternoon to an invasion from outer space.

Dr. Grant Wynn of the State Health Department, informed of the phenomenon Friday, said he had no guess as to what the substance might be.

On the 18th, two Ogallalo, Nebraska, youths reported seeing a lighted object cross the sky. Its speeds varied from 25 mph to about 400 mph. Additional reports of flying saucers came in from a Wyoming and North Dakota. The state police were called out on a number of occasions to investigate the strange forms in the night sky.

On Sunday, October 21, Air Force Lt. Col. Lawrence J. Tacker appeared on the WOR-TV program "Meet the Authors." Along with interviewer Walter Kiernan were panelists Dr. John Ubell and Willy Ley. The book discussed was Tacker's "**Flying Saucers and the U.S. Air Force.**" The half-hour show was extremely one-sided, in that all concerned were vehemently anti-saucer. The only sightings covered were the Kenneth Arnold report in 1947 and the Washington, D.C. radar incidents in 1952. Perhaps the only good thing for us believers was that Willy Ley admitted it was possible for beings from another planet to be visiting us, though he doubted very much that such a thing had ever taken place.

Apparently the citizens of Sidney, Nebraska, didn't view the Tacker show, for on the following day a large, fiery object that swooped low over the countryside and headed west was observed by at least eight persons.

INSIDE THE SAUCERS - MR. UFOS TEENAGE YEARS

Few reports came in to us in November, but, on the first of the month, George D. Fawcett of Woburn, Massachusetts, interviewed Mr. Charles F. Kirk, 20, a machinist and carpenter for the Wells Machine Company. It seems that between 2 and 2:10 P.M., a streamlined, egg-shaped object which was golden-orange in color and in appearance resembled an egg cut in half hovered for eight or nine minutes in the eastern sky. Mr. Kirk estimated that it was 40 feet long, 30 feet wide, 15 feet high, at an altitude of about 2000 feet.

He reported that the UFO produced a band of light around the building on which he was working. He also stated that the object, which was flat underneath with a black band near its lower edge, seemed to have a projection or periscope hanging about ten feet from underneath it. Mr. Kirk reported he thought it was "taking pictures of the earth below," due to a clicking sound he could hear every 15 seconds or so. This, he stated to Mr. Fawcett, was the only audible sound. The UFO then rose and disappeared at lightning speed. The area was checked by a Geiger counter later that evening by Woburn Civil Defense worker, Mr. L.C. Anstery, who found a slight increase in the background radiation.

On November 13, mysterious flashes were seen in the night sky over Atlanta, Georgia, and two other southeastern cities. The Eglin Air Force Base of Mobile, Alabama, said the flashes could have been caused by a chemical released from an Astrobee rocket; however, no concrete evidence was offered.

Jack Bartlett, a member of INS, wrote that a mysterious shockwave and a saucer-shaped UFO were reported in a wide area around metropolitan San Diego, California, on November 15. A Chula Vista policeman, Ralph G. Breitsch, said he saw a fiery-tailed object cross the southern sky from east to west and then plunge seaward. Many residents in the area complained of windows rattling and other such phenomena which the police diagnosed as something close to a sonic boom. Mrs. John Brown and Del Mar reported a glowing saucer-shaped object that appeared to hang in midair over the San Diego River bed. The Navy and Air Force said they had no unusual flight activities in the area at the time of the reports.

Mr. Kurt Warren, a skydiving enthusiast, on Sunday afternoon, November 25, went up for about a mile and a half jump. Afterwards he was told that all the observers on the ground had spotted a shining object just before the jump. He himself did not see any unusual object, though. Flight schedules were checked, and it was found that no aircraft were allowed in the area during jumping runs.

Just a few days later, two boys in Alabama reported that they had observed strange lights on the shoreline and in a deep forest area of the state. It seems Alabama has had its share of unusual objects. Evidence of this is seen by viewing past reports: On October 24 a mysterious object was sighted over the central part of the state. Many people called various official and state government organizations after they had witnessed the UFO. A newscast stated that jet fighters were sent up to investigate, but they saw nothing; and the weather bureau said that it was probably only a lost balloon. But if it was, how could it have outmaneuvered a jet traveling at over 500 mph with the latest type of radar?

Now we come to December, which is the beginning of the holiday season but ostensibly not the season to view UFOs, it seems. However, the month began with a rash of reports that as usual turned out merely to be lost balloons, birds, meteorites and local rig-a-ma-role. One impressive sighting, though, did take place in Monterey County, California, on December 14. It seems that a big silver ball of fire that failed to make a blip on Air Force radars and that possibly set a hovering record for flying saucers – 4:27 A.M.to 8:20 A.M. – was sighted south of the community. "I was checking the thermometer on the front porch – it was 54 – when I saw it, a big white object, not red at all, in the east," said Greenfield Constable Rod Miller, a veteran of eight years' experience.

"Then patrolman Nick Heinz of the Greenfield Police Department telephoned me and asked if I had seen it. He said he would come over with his binoculars. We watched it until 8:20 in the morning, when it was covered by one of those little shirttail clouds," the constable added.

Miller said it was his first sighting of an unidentified flying object. However, he was not alone in his experience. Police officers in Monterey, King City, and Soledad reported seeing a similar object.

A spokesman at Hamilton Air Force Base said the station radars had failed to record any unusual flying bodies. He said a meteor shower had been expected in the area, but added that a full report would be forwarded to the technical information center at Wright-Patterson Air Force Base in Dayton, Ohio.

The sighting was covered in many newspapers and was partly printed in the *San Francisco Examiner* on the following day, December 15. The same report appeared in the Chronicle, which said that 35 persons reported a bright light high in the sky, changing color from flame-red to white and pulsating with a kind of halo. It alternately hovered and moved at high speed.

What this year has brought will be discussed in the ensuing chapters of this book. Much is yet to be learned, but with the help and guidance of all, a great deal can be accomplished in a short period of time. One top-level researcher, who will remain nameless, has given his time and energy to see that there is a unity among UFO groups. He has spent many a dollar on this project and has gathered together under one banner many interested groups which are willing to investigate seriously all reports of UFOs.

Being set up at this moment are plans for the International UFOlogical Year. Most UFO groups don't have the time and the equipment for serious investigation of the subject. For the most part they are run on spare time, which means they can't possibly inform other groups of what they are doing.

Because there is so little cooperation between UFOlogists, many disputes have arisen on misunderstandings. This indeed poses quite a serious problem. It has come to the point at which one has to subscribe to ten different publications to get the information so essentially needed. One way to cure this situation has been suggested, that being a joint exchange of bulletins and information received among all groups.

A weekly bulletin will be published by the United Saucer Council of Ohio and sent to all groups. This bulletin will contain the reports of the different organizations and of individual participation. At the end of the year, it has been suggested that all this information be published jointly and under one cover. It is stressed that this is not going to be used as one big group, but as a group of individual organizations exchanging information. This "year" will be 15 months long, from March 1, 1963 to May 1, 1964.

With ideas like the above, the UFO mystery will not be a mystery for long. UNITY is the key word for progress. If only this had been done 15 or even 10 years ago, we would be much closer to the final answer.

Some groups have already shown interest in the International UFOlogical Year and other projects like it. However, there still remains a vast populace who wish to have nothing to do with UFO group unity, for the reason that they want all their information to be top secret until it is possible for them to print it at their convenience. What does this all add up to? UFOLOGY'S DEATH!

So let us prove in the coming year that UFO research is a science, one that should be investigated to the utmost!

FOREIGN SIGHTINGS OF 1962

By Jerome Clark

1962 will probably be recorded as the most important UFO year since 1957, not so much for the number of sightings (although there were many) as for their quality and nature. In many ways, 1962 proved even more important than any other year since the inception of the saucer enigma over sixteen years ago, for never before have so many significant – and in some cases ominous – incidents have been chronicled. Nor have there been so many meaningful clues to the nature and purpose of the mysterious discs.

Not all reports were this important, of course, but they were interesting nevertheless. Sightings were recorded all over the world, as always, but particularly in South America, where the most astonishing took place. A few UFOs remained in England during the early part of the year, apparently left over from the "flap" that country experienced during the summer of 1961. Immediately following England was Italy, which reported several seemingly authentic contacts. Other sightings took place in scattered locales without any apparent pattern, with the possible exception of the Soviet Union. Since 1961, various rumors have emanated from behind the Iron Curtain to the effect that UFO flights of unprecedented proportions have overflown parts of Russia, resulting in Pravda's denial of the reality of the phenomena as "capitalistic imaginings." Unfortunately, only a handful of reports have managed to leak out, so the extent of the visitation remains unknown and undoubtedly will remain this way until the Communist leaders change their absurd, self-contradictory policy. Even then (assuming such an event ever does take place), it is possible that details will remain sketchy, for most outsiders are not allowed to know the internal affairs of the Soviet Union.

GREAT BRITAIN

On January 3, several persons residing in Worcestershire, England, witnessed a strange "comet-like" object which descended from the sky. According to one of them, Alfred John Davies, a gardener, "It was the most wonderful sight I have seen in my life. It seemed to be about three yards long with a shimmering ball of bright green light on the end. I only saw it for a moment, but it seemed to disappear over the North Hill of the Malverns. Just before I lost sight of it, it exploded, the ball coming away from the tail. It looked to me like a comet."

Authorities stated that, while other sightings in the past in the area had, in fact, been caused by weather balloons, the latest report could not be so easily explained, as none was in the area at the time.

The London Times for January 15 reported an odd incident in which "a suspected meteorite" had caused a great explosion in the skies over Whitehaven, Cumberland. A large greenish rock, reeking of sulfur, was found on the open grounds in front of a chemical factory in Kells. An officer of the British Astronomical Association, notified of the report, expressed skepticism of certain parts of the story, notably the peculiar smell and the fact that it was too hot to touch. This is not typical of meteorites, he said.

One can't help noticing a certain resemblance to UFO phenomena in this incident because "sulfur" or "rotten-egg" odors are often reported in connection with flying saucers. Is it possible that a UFO exploded over Whitehaven, and that the "meteorite" in reality is a piece of residue from it?

The most important single sighting from England occurred on a Sunday morning in late February or early March. A 14-year-old boy named Alexander Birch of Mosborough, Sheffield, was standing in a field in the Birch garden with two friends, David Brownshaw and Stuart Dixon, when they noticed five strange aerial machines of a dull black color hovering above them at an altitude of about 600 feet. After the first seven seconds, several bright blobs of light appeared behind the objects, making viewing difficult. Fortunately, about then the young Birch thought of his camera and managed to snap a picture with a cheap box model that he had with him before the UFOs disappeared with the characteristic "terrific speed." Tenure of the sighting was between 12 and 14 seconds.

The photograph was studied by competent authorities, who concluded it was genuine. Officials of the English Air Ministry expressed a great deal of interest in the case, and Mr. Birch and his son were invited to London so that the picture could be evaluated. The following is his account, as quoted in the March-April, 1963, *"Flying Saucer Review"*:

"We arrived at the Air Ministry at approximately 12:30 P.M. on August 27, 1962, along with a Yorkshire Post reporter, and were taken with a great shroud of security to see a Mr. P. H. White, with whom we had to leave all the evidence, the negative, the prints and the camera, for them to examine. He asked Alex if he had enjoyed the train journey, and, after the reporter had left, asked him several questions relating the flying saucers, their size and what they were like and how long they were in sight. The enquiry finished for the day, and he asked me to bring my son back next morning at 11 A.M.

"We stayed overnight at a very nice hotel as guests of the Yorkshire Post. We then visited the Air Ministry the following morning (August 28, 1962) at the stated time of appointment, but before we entered the Press tried to take a picture of my son Alex and myself entering up the steps of the Air Ministry building. This is when we felt the real whiplash of security attached to my endeavor of trying to keep an open mind on this business. We were immediately surrounded by guards in uniform and plain-clothes security men. My boy was sincerely frightened to death. However, after the head security man had consulted on the phone with Mr. White, the Press was allowed to take the photograph 30 minutes afterwards.

"We then were signed in along with a reporter from the Yorkshire Post and taken to Mr. P. H. White's room. When we entered, Mr. P. H. White immediately stood to his feet and asked what on earth was the Yorkshire Post reporter doing coming in with us. The reporter said he was under the impression of the previous day that Mr. White knew he was accompanying us. Then Mr. White, in front of two other high-ranking security men, promptly denied this, and the two security men entered and ushered the reporter out of the building.

"By this time, my boy was sick with fear and then, when the interview began, they waved young Alex from my side and asked him to sit at the opposite side of the room. Then the three officials started what I will call a 'brainwash.' They kept on asking him wasn't it any reflection that he saw and what was the weather like, what were the formations of cloud, was there snow on the ground. Those questions they must have repeated at least 30 times. Then what was the color of the object and for how long were they visible to the boys and in what direction the objects went. They then had my boy draw on paper size about 20 inches by 14 inches all the roads and mark where all the towns were in that area and the exact spot where he saw and photographed the saucers. The questions went on endlessly for three hours without a break and the only comment they made to me was that they could find no fault in the negatives or prints or the camera.

"I tried to press them further but they wouldn't say anything more. Then, on October 17, 1962, they wrote me saying that when Alex took the photograph there were ice particles in the atmosphere and in the Sheffield area smoke and haze were present and generally cloud formations at various altitudes were many and varied; pockets of warm air rising from the city would have caused temperature inversions and under these conditions reflected and refracted light can cause peculiar effects in the sky, and this is what they thought attracted Alex and his two friends' attention and they may have photographed these effects. What utter rubbish! I am utterly disgusted with this report. These three boys saw those flying saucers hovering and then making off at a terrific speed, and, what's more, photographed them. I myself was a nonbeliever in these objects, and may I say that since visiting the Air Ministry I am firmly convinced that we are being visited by flying saucers of other planets and, what is more, the Air Ministry knows also but won't admit it."

During the early morning hours of February 9, a Luton, Bedfordshire, man named Ronald Wildman was driving toward Swansea delivering a new Vauxhall car. About 3:30 he approached a deserted road near Ivinghoe when he saw a 40-foot object hovering 20 or 30 feet in the air.

"As soon as I came within 20 yards of it, the power of my car changed – it dropped right down to 20 mph," Wildman claimed. He shifted the auto into second gear and put his foot on the accelerator, but nothing happened. "I had my headlights full on, and although the engine lost revs., the lights did not fade."

The UFO, which was shaped like a huge disc with a row of "vents" on the bottom, flew ahead of Wildman by at least 20 feet, doing so for about 200 yards. Then it started to come lower, and, as it did, a sort of whitish haze appeared around it – "like a halo around the moon," said the witness. "It veered off to the right at a terrific speed and then vanished." In doing so, "it brushed particles of frost from the treetops to my windscreen. It was definitely a solid object because the reflection of my headlights was thrown back from it."

On March 14 a glowing red object crashed through a coach window of the Nottingham-Newark diesel train at Carlton. One of the passengers was hit by flying glass but was not hurt.

According to Richard Pannell of Trinity Road, Newark, "I saw a glowing red object about the size of a cricket ball traveling at great speed in a wavering flight towards the train. When it hit the coach, there was a noise like an explosion."

A railroad official expressed puzzlement, stating that if it had been a meteorite or something thrown at the train, it was strange that "nothing was found in the coach, no stone or anything like that."

The following report was published in the *Birmingham Mail* for May 16:

AIRLINE PILOT SEES GLOBE FLYING AT 500 MPH

Captain Gordon Pendleton, of Aer Lingus, said last night that while flying his four-engine Viscount airliner yesterday at 17,000 feet from Cork to Brussels, he saw a globe-shaped object streaking towards him at more than 500 mph.

"I have never seen anything like it," he said. "The object passed nearly 3,000 feet underneath me. I have always been skeptical about flying saucers. Now I don't know what to think.

"If it had been a plane, I would have seen the wings. It did not appear to have any."

None of the 60 passengers, nor the two stewardesses, saw the object.

An Aer Lingus official said in London that the UFO was seen 35 miles south of Bristol and was also seen by the plane's first officer, Peter Murray. He described it as "large, round, brown, smaller than their plane, and with antennae."

An interesting incident giving further evidence for the possibility that UFOs have undersea bases is described in the *Durham Evening Gazette* for June first. According to the newspaper, "An intensive air and sea search was going on near Blackhall Rocks this afternoon after a plane was reported to have dived into the sea. The drama began about noon when a man working at Blackhall Colliery telephoned the police after seeing 'a flash across the sky and into the sea.'"

A lifeboat was launched and two aircraft were dispatched to the scene. Nothing was found, however. The Air Ministry denied that any Royal Air Force planes were missing.

A spectacular series of sightings occurred over Sheffield between August 19 and 30, the most important of which resulted in a movie being taken by Walter Revill, a cutlery worker. Revill told the Yorkshire Post that, while standing in his garden, he saw a low-flying UFO. "It seemed to be made up of two saucers, one over the other, with a sort of platform in between and made of glass," he stated. The object, which remained visible for about 15 minutes, had a "searchlight" emanating from it and made no noise.

Revill hurried inside his house, getting a movie camera, with which he exposed ten feet of film. His comment about the whole affair is typical of that expressed by most saucer witnesses: "I have never believed in flying saucers before, but I am absolutely convinced this was one."

The sighting was confirmed by three other persons, all of whom expressed similar opinions.

(For a complete account of the Sheffield reports, see the November-December, 1962, "*Flying Saucer Review*.")

Next to the Birch story, the most publicized British report was a story from Duncannon, Ireland, describing the crash of a mysterious basketball-sized object. The explosion blew a three-foot hole in a Duncannon field and, when the military were notified, the area was roped off from passersby. No further details have been forthcoming.

On the afternoon of December 19, 21-year-old Harold Threlkeld, a resident of Ings, Staveley, reported seeing a "scout-ship" similar to that first photographed by George Adamski and later by Stephen Darbishire. According to the account, Threlkeld was driving a van looking for Christmas holly when he stopped half a mile from Elterwater, and began to walk up the fellside on the right side of the road. While walking up, he heard a "continuous buzzing sound" which became louder and louder until finally he looked around him to find the source.

"Then I happened to glance up again and saw a huge great thing in the sky, like a disc or saucer upside down," he later stated. The UFO, hovering about 700 feet in the air and at a 45 degree angle, was a light blue color, measured from 60 to 70 feet, and had a dome on the top; on the bottom was a three-ball landing gear. "I could see through the dome and see that there were something like tables or benches inside." After Threlkeld had watched the phenomenon for about two and a half minutes, it shot off at the typical "terrific speed."

THE EUROPEAN CONTINENT

Important sightings on the European continent were spectacularly lacking in 1962 – with one exception, Italy. In that county a number of apparently authentic contact claims were reported in the press. They are summarized below.

On April 10, a worker named Mario Zuccala was walking by the forest of Cidinella, Val di Pesa, about 9:25 P.M., going home. The sky was clear, and many stars were visible. While crossing a small canal that flows across the street, he was suddenly hit by a sharp gust of wind which almost threw him off his feet. Turning, he was shocked to see a UFO – shaped like "two bowls put one on top of the other" – hovering a few feet above the Earth. As he watched it, it began to move and passed over him and then settled to Earth, resting about two and a half meters in the air. A cylinder came out of the craft's bottom and touched the ground. Then a door, from which an intense light emanated, opened, and two beings, dressed in a kind of "armor" and measuring about four and a half feet in height, emerged and gently forced Zuccala into the object, where another voice, speaking ostensibly from an amplifier and in Italian, gave him a message. "At the fourth moon we shall come at one o'clock in the morning. We shall give notice of this to another person in order to confirm that which you have seen is true," it said. Then Zucalla was led out. The time was approximately 9:45 P.M.

An even stranger account was described by a 20-year-old man named Roberto Peregozo of Verona. He claims that, during the evening hours of June 26, he was sitting up with his sister and mother smoking when they noticed a slivery disc maneuvering in the sky outside. It remained visible for about an hour, after which the two women retired. Roberto went to his own room.

About 3 A.M. the daughter woke up complaining of intense cold. "And then I saw a greenish fluctuating light invade the whole room," she told the newspaper *La Domenncia del Corriere*. "Before I could recover from my astonishment, I saw appear, two paces from my bed and in the rectangular opening of the window, an incorporeal being in human form, but with only the outlines hazily defined. The rest of it was transparent. It had an enormous close-shaven head. Although impalpable and, maybe, weightless, I could nevertheless see it, gigantic, with its huge legs and its huge hands extended towards me as if it intended to carry me off. It was motionless and only its hands brushed me. It had no particular odor."

At this point, she began to scream, waking her mother, who fainted upon seeing the creature. Just then Roberto rushed into the room, where he beheld it. Almost immediately the form began to diminish, passed through a window, and "disappeared in a flash, just like a TV set when it goes out." The cold remained, however.

So unnerved by the whole experience were they that the family have since moved to a cottage in the country.

Yet another weird occurrence was reported in the Italian press. It seems that on December 17, a Milan policeman, Francesco Rizzi, was patrolling around 2:20 A.M. when he heard a peculiar swishing noise. Puzzled, he turned around, there to see a flying saucer hovering about three feet above the ground. In describing it, Rizzi stated, "It was of a clear metal, perhaps of aluminum with silvery reflections on it; its diameter may have been 12 to 15 feet. On top there was a turret around which were a number of domed windows, lighted. I was paralyzed and tried hard to believe my own eyes, when suddenly the noise stopped."

At the saucer's bottom a door opened, and a three-foot being, wearing "a kind of luminous overall," emerged and beckoned to the frightened officer, who was unable to move. Then "another man jumped out of the disc, submerged in a blue haze. With a commanding gesture, he made a sign to the other to re-enter the disc. Suddenly the door closed behind them both, the swishing noise again started, and the disc disappeared in a cloud of white smoke."

NOTE: Apparently confirming the story cited above is the description of the "swishing noise," for on December 9 and 11, 1954, two UFO landings were reported in Rio Grande do Sul, and in each case the witness, an uneducated farmer, reported similar sounds emanating from the craft. In the first incident, Olmiro da Costa e Rosa stated, "I was mowing in a French-bean and maize field when I heard a strange noise, resembling that of a sewing machine." The source of the noise proved to be a flying saucer. And in the second case, Pedro Morais said, "I saw a strange object suspended in the air, hovering, making a noise like that of a sewing machine." The stories are particularly convincing because the two men, though they lived within half a mile of each other, neither knew each other nor were cognizant of the other's sighting. (See "Report from Brazil," by Dr. Olavo Fontes, in *"Fantastic Universe"* for August, 1958, for complete details.)

It almost goes without saying that a sewing machine makes a "swishing" sound.

SOUTH AMERICA

An extremely large and important flap took place in all of South America during 1962, particularly in Argentina and Brazil. Latest information indicates that even now (mid-1963) it has not totally died out. Unfortunately, as yet only two American saucer magazines (The *APRO Bulletin* and *Saucer News*) have published the sightings in any detail; therefore, we are grateful to them for the information presented in the following paragraphs. We are only going to describe the most spectacular reports, as most of the others may be obtained from the two periodicals mentioned.

In early May the Argentine Air Force investigated a report of a UFO landing in La Pampa province. A rancher and his wife claimed to have seen two robot-like creatures emerge from the machine, only to re-enter it upon noting they were being observed. Authorities who later came to the scene confirmed that the grass where the craft had allegedly landed was singed in a peculiar manner. Additional confirmation came from the fact that the woman had to be hospitalized from shock.

On July 26, about 8:30 P.M., 17-year-old Ricardo Mieres was riding his motorcycle down an abandoned road when the headlight hit an odd-looking being standing on the left side of the road. Supposedly against his will, the motorcycle moved to within three inches of the creature, which stood six feet tall and had a three-eyed head shaped like a "melon." The thing grabbed Meires' scarf and began to walk away in the manner of a robot, and, as it did so, left deep tracks in the dirt. A peculiar craft is said to have been hovering nearby.

On August 20 or 21, a doctor named Gazcue was driving, with his wife, toward Parana, Argentina, when he saw a flying saucer. On the ground were two six-foot beings, with light hair and large eyes (apparently similar to Adamski's supposed Venusians); they wore luminous objects on their foreheads and were motioning towards the couple. However, Dr. Gazcue became frightened and immediately accelerated ahead. His wife suffered from nervous shock afterwards.

As incredible as these incidents may be, the most fantastic of all came from Brazil. The whole astonishing series of events leading up to Rivalino Mafra da Silva's disappearance began on August 17. On that date, Mafra was walking toward his house when he saw two odd creatures digging a hole. The beings, which were three feet tall, fled when they saw Mafra approaching them. Immediately thereafter, a mysterious hat-shaped object arose from behind the bushes into which they had run.

Three days later, on the 20th, Mafra and his three sons, Raimundo, 12, Fatimo, 6, and Dirceu, 2, were in bed (Mafra was a widower), when they heard a sound as of people walking around the room. In the dim light, the oldest boy and his father could see what appeared to be a queer shadow – "not shaped like a human being" – which was not touching the floor. After gliding over toward where the two smaller boys lay sleeping, it left the building by going out the front door, which was closed. Afterwards, voices could be heard from outside, saying, "This one looks like Rivalino."

Mafra, startled, called out, "Who goes there?"

Getting no answer, he arose and entered the other room, where the voices began speaking again. They asked him if he was, in fact, Rivalino, to which he replied in the affirmative, and then he went back to bed.

The voices were not through with him, though, for they began to threaten him, saying that they would kill him. When he began praying aloud, they told him that to do so was useless.

The next morning Raimundo went outside to get his father's horse, where he saw, lying a few feet from the door, two metallic balls. One was black, while the other was black and white. A humming sound was emitted by them, and fire was flickering through an opening in the objects.

At this point the father came out, obviously distraught from the activities of the night before, and when he saw the two machines on the ground, he stared as though hypnotized. Warning Raimundo to stay back, he walked toward them and stopped about six feet away.

"At that moment," the boy later told investigators, "the two objects, which resembled big balls, joined up into one, sending out lots of smoke and dust so that the sky was blackened with it. Without rising from the ground, but making a queer noise, the thing crept towards Daddy. Daddy was covered by the strange cloud of dust, which was the color of sunset (yellowish), and he disappeared in the whirlwind produced by the objects. I went after Daddy in the middle of the cloud of dust, which had a strange smell, but I couldn't see anything. I called out to Daddy, but got no answer. At once the dust vanished, as if by magic, leaving no marks whatever on the hard earth, and it looked as though the place had been swept with a broom."

Raimundo searched carefully for the next few days, but found nothing – not so much as a trace of his father.

When authorities studied the story, they were unable to get the boy to deny the account. A number of tests, some of them quite cruel, failed to shake him.

Other evidence for the reality of the incident was forthcoming. It developed that about a week before Rivalino's disappearance three men had observed two balls flying low over the victim's house, flashing a light. Said one of the men, "I know nothing about the disappearance of Sr. Rivalino, but I did see two strange objects in the sky over Duas Pontes. From the description of the objects given by the son of the missing man, I have the impression that they were the same as those seen by me."

When reading the account of the disappearance for the first time, I experienced a vague feeling that the story was not completely without precedent. After a thorough re-reading, I remembered, when, in his testimony, Raimundo had said that his father "disappeared in a WHIRLWIND (my italics) produced by the objects." The Old Testament book of II Kings, second chapter, eleventh verse, describes a famous pilgrimage made by Elijah and Elisha: "And it came to pass, as they still went on, and talked, that, behold, there appeared a chariot of fire, and horses of fire, and parted them both asunder; and Elijah went up BY A WHIRLWIND (again, my italics) into heaven." Was Elijah also kidnapped by a UFO?

Besides the Mafra affair, there were two other lesser known abductions in Brazil. The first occurred in mid-September near Barcelos when three rubber tree plantation workers saw a slivery disc hovering over a river. Upon reporting the occurrence, they were thrown into jail by the mayor, who said that they were spreading rumors "to prejudice his administration." Unconvinced, a police officer made an investigation, concluding that the UFO was responsible for the disappearances of 17 chickens, six pigs and two cows, all of which had vanished on the night the unknown machine first appeared.

The second abduction took place on September 16, near Vila Conceicao, Amazonas. After refereeing a soccer game, Telemaco Xavier was walking home through a nearby forest when he vanished. Searchers combed the countryside all night and well through the day, succeeding only in finding the missing man's whistle. Finally, however, a peculiar story was told by a rubber tree worker, who said that on the night of the 16th he had seen a glowing circular craft which emitted sparks come in to land near a clearing where the referee was walking. Three "men" came out of the UFO and attempted to haul Xavier into it, but the official fought bravely until finally he was overcome and taken away.

An on-the-spot investigation revealed signs of a struggle, substantiating the story. Concluded the Rio de Janeiro newspapers, "It seems evident, beyond any doubt, that Mr. Telemaco Xavier was kidnapped by a flying disc."

Before closing, we mention one last incident worthy of note. Complete details such as the date are not available, but we present what is known: Three Argentinian astro-students are said to have photographed a disc-shaped object over Cordoba, the veracity of which has been testified to by camera experts. Moreover, the original sighting was also attested to by other persons who watched the object from the airport.

CONCLUSION

What is the meaning of the saucer events of 1962? As we pointed out in the introduction to this article, this past year has been proven extremely important, for now the UFOs seem to be coming more and more out into the open and their moves are bolder – more close range observations, more landings and contacts (at least apparently authentic contacts, not at all like those of the Adamski, Bethurum, King, etc. varieties), and abductions and other hostile acts.

Recently there has been a feeling among some researchers that the saucer enigma is drawing to its inevitable climax. Even Dr. Olavo T. Fontes, probably one of the two or three most brilliant men in the field, has expressed such an opinion.

The coming of the UFOs can be correlated with the incredible advance of technology that has been witnessed since the end of World War II, particularly in the fields of atomic energy and space travel. More than anything else, the objects have shown interest in these, as evidenced by the Oak Ridge and White Sands cases a number of years ago, and, more recently, those from Cape Canaveral and still others in outer space – UFOs following the Echo and Sputnik satellites as well as the man-in-space probes of the past two or three years – and the 1952 flap – during the hydrogen bomb tests – and the 1957 flap – shortly after the first artificial satellite launchings – and the 1962 flap – during the many manned orbit shots. One gets the idea that the UFO intelligences are waiting for our really spectacular efforts, perhaps the explosion of a nuclear bomb on the surface of the moon or the first manned expeditions there and beyond.

Are they afraid of our warlike ways? Do they fear we will take our cold and hot wars into space with us? That may be, but I am inclined to doubt it, for in studying the actions of the UFOs toward human beings, one finds that in the majority of cases it is they – not we – who are the aggressors. There is another, more deeply seated reason. Reviewing the available data, the researchers are led to the conclusion that there is more than one force – one intelligence – behind the UFOs just on the basis of landing reports alone. Elsewhere I have written that one of the major flaws in UFOlogical thinking is that "the UFOs are all manifestations of one, and only one, certain phenomenon."

The truth is that there are several forces, and that they are in conflict – a kind of cosmic "cold war." The Earth is being closely observed as it moves on to become an extraterrestrial power. Our efforts are watched with puzzled reticence because someday we shall be powerful enough, if left untouched, to tip the scales of power.

Our planet is not the only one, but it is probably among the more important of those presently emerging. What is happening now, what has been happening since the end of World War II, is only a small part in a universal drama.

An example of this can be had if we think of the present power struggle going on between the United States and the Soviet Union. The West idealistically attempts to sway the emerging nations of Africa and Asia to its side by peaceful means, while the Eastern powers subvert them in their efforts to bring them to their side. This illustration explains, for instance, why some UFOs are seemingly friendly and others are more or less hostile.

The climax to the saucer saga may or may not come in the near future. Only time will answer this question, but it is safe to say that it is in the foreseeable future.

NOTE ON SOURCES: The factual portions of the above article are based upon material appearing in the following publications: *"Flying Saucer Review"* (England), *"The APRO Bulletin," "The NJAAP UFO News Bulletin," "The INS Report,"* and *"Saucer News."*

COMMENT ON THE UFO MYSTERY

By Timothy Green Beckley

IT is difficult to say exactly when the UFOs began visiting our Earth. If we check the records of Charles Fort, Harold T. Wilkins, and others, however, we can, with a fair amount of certainty; state these objects began their observations around the year 1640. But even before then there were many reports of strange balls of fire in the sky; these can be linked with reports of fireballs today. The possibility that UFOs are of extraterrestrial origin has been debated for over 15 years, with some researchers maintaining that such is very unlikely and others taking an opposite viewpoint, some even claiming contact with the craft and their occupants.

But should these phenomena prove to be terrestrial, many persons will be in for a shock, for the objects may in the long run prove dangerous to us. If they do come from the Earth, where are they built? Certainly not in the United States or Russia, because secrets of this magnitude cannot easily be hidden from enemy intelligence agents. Just where, then, does this lead us?

It is a known fact that during the Second World War Germany was rapidly developing secret weapons, one of which was a saucer-shaped craft. After Hitler was defeated and fled to Argentina (he wasn't really killed), his followers, who numbered in the thousands, still continued to carry out his every command. One of them was to build this strange craft.

We, of course, have the problem of how the Germans got a hold of such a craft or even the plans for one. Recalling some of the unexplained events of World War II, we are reminded of the foo-fighters and also of another phenomenon – little men. It seems that in the spring of 1942 a strange craft landed and was captured by the Germans. Inside the ship were three small humanoids, each weighing about 98 pounds and averaging in height four feet.

In this way the Germans found a weapon that could easily have won the war for them, but Hitler wanted power too fast and would not wait for invention to be perfected.

During the late 1940s and early 1950s experiments were still being carried out in secret in Hitler's secret hideaway. Many sightings were being recorded on radar at this time, and the little men were just coming into the picture full-scale. Frank Scully's book **"Behind the Flying Saucers"** aroused the interest of the public, making it believe the objects were interplanetary. Of course, the United States government had no idea what was happening until Project Saucer closed up, changing its name to Project Blue Book.

Another question now arises, that being how the passengers of these craft could live through the incredible speeds reported by countless saucer witnesses. The answer is that more than one group of UFOs is truly interplanetary. Their bodies have been changed over a period of time in order to use to greater advantage the Earth's gravity. Their experiments can be reviewed again by reading Scully's 1950 book. Earlier, Kenneth Arnold had sighted his now famous nine saucers, which appeared to him as if they were skipping over water; in actuality, they were pulling instead of pushing the Earth's atmosphere. The pull of gravity was too much and, in turn, killed a number of these hairy, four-foot creatures.

Take the case of Captain Thomas Mantell, who, over the state of Kentucky, mysteriously plunged to his death chasing the Planet Venus. However, the facts are different. After a more thorough investigation it was discovered that the Planet Venus wasn't visible at the time. Moreover, the object seen by witnesses on the ground was much larger. Ostensibly, Mantell either knew too much or was trying to find out more and in doing so met his death. One researcher says he has information that Mantell's last words were, "I CAN SEE WINDOWS! MY GOD, THERE'S PEOPLE IN IT!" This startling statement was given to the researcher by a man who did some FBI work and whose reliability was confirmed by Desmond Leslie.

These celestial craft may come from almost anywhere. They might just as well come from 100,000 miles (as suggested by the strange "Vero Edition" of M.K. Jessup's **"The Case for the UFO"**) or one hundred billion miles.

Many leading scientists have taken a stand either one way or another regarding possible extraterrestrial life. Dr. Harlow Shapley, former Director of Harvard College Observatory, has stated that the universe probably contains millions of inhabited planets containing beings more advanced than we. Dr. Freeman J. Dyson of the Institute for Advanced Study at Princeton, New Jersey, says it is an "overwhelming probability" that beings exist on other planets, and that these creatures are probably more technologically advanced. One Russian scientist says that he believes there is a great possibility of life on the moon, but that this life would be only in a primitive stage. Dr. George Gaylord Simpson of Harvard University had this to say when asked about the possibility of life elsewhere: "If the universe is infinite, there must be an infinite number of planets in it which exactly duplicate the Earth, all the inhabitants, their history. If, however, the universe is finite and not infinite, as many astronomers believe, then the chances of finding manlike creatures anywhere else are zero." Indiana University zoologist Hermann J. Muller stated to newsmen: "Intelligent beings on other planets will have senses such as hearing and sight but will probably be as different from humans as a lobster is."

To go back to the Germans and their craft, we must keep in mind that all the information cannot be exact, as few details are present. One must piece the puzzle together in his own mind to come out with the correct answer.

U.S. AIR FORCE SECRECY AND THE INTERNATIONAL BANKERS

Throughout this volume you will be reading more about the International Bankers and their part in the Bender Mystery. It has been reported that the Bender book would deal in full with these agents, but a last minute ducking-out by both Gray Barker and Albert K. Bender prevented the original manuscript from ever being published. This might even be the reason for the long delay in getting the book released and sent out to the public.

Most modern saucer researchers insist the U.S. government and the Air Force in particular are withholding information from the public that might help solve the UFO mystery. In fact, the only researcher who will uphold the Air Force's views is "*Saucer News*" editor James W. Moseley. Mr. Moseley is one of only two persons who, as civilians, have been permitted to inspect the files at Wright-Patterson Air Force Base in Dayton, Ohio, the home of the Air Force's Project Blue Book. (The only other researcher was Thomas Camella, in 1954.)

Organizations like NICAP are always pressing for open Congressional hearings on the subject. In the past they have always been thwarted by a wall of incredible secrecy, a wall that gets thicker every day, we are told.

Apparently it has not occurred to many persons that perhaps the Air Force is not in charge of UFO information, and perhaps any data that are received by it come from a higher source.

Reverend Frank Stranges claims that during a trip to Washington, D.C., he was invited to the Pentagon so that he might interview a visitor from the Planet Venus. He tells his story in his booklet "***My Friend from Beyond Earth***."

The International Bankers can once again be brought into the picture. It seems from past records that those mysterious visitors from space are none other than agents of the Bankers themselves. You will remember Albert K. Bender's statement that his visitors wanted their mission to remain a secret, by planting agents to throw groups and individuals off the track, Bender being one of those persons himself. The story of Al Bender will be detailed in another chapter.

This organization known as the International Bankers is located in all countries but seems to be centered mainly around England and India. In the February-March, 1957, issue of "*Saucer News*," the following letter was printed:

"Here in Bombay, there is much dismay among members of our club, called the 'Vimanians,' over numerous letters which have been sent to people showing interest in the Vimanas. The few copies of your rival editor's '**They Knew Too Much About Flying Saucers**' made an immediate impression on us. We would like you to know that we, too, have experienced for some time these visitations from taciturn but menacing young men of apparently Northern-Asian or Western race-type.

"Simultaneously, we have received polite but sinister letters from the very 'International Bankers' whose name figures so much these days from the Occidental side of the UFO world. We are not racially as 'hardboiled' as you people seem to be, and therefore we are genuinely distressed to find ourselves in receipt of these strangely-phrased threatening letters. Some of the letters have been quite offensive and all that I have seen have been worded very peculiarly in most uncommon English.

"The men who have called at the homes of us 'Vimanians' have made us feel most uncomfortable by constantly referring to our nationalistic difficulties and our relationship with the U.S.S.R. They do not appear to be Communist in their outlook but, during the late British regime, they would certainly have been classified as 'agents provocateurs' and their occasional suggestions would most definitely have been condemned as seditious.

"The letters that I have seen as well as the few common details which I have gleaned from those who have not been too badly scared to discuss their 'Visitors' contain a strong element of interest in happenings in the region of Tibet. From Pakistan I have heard of one or more of these strangers asking questions concerning the political situation on the borders of Afghanistan, Waziristan and Nepal.

"The strangest thing about this mystery is that, at no time, have there been any direct references to on the part of these questioners to their own country. In fact it has been suggested that they do not live on this Earth at all but that they are agents from outer space. To some degree they are exceptionally well-informed, but sometimes on matters of commonest common knowledge they are definitely more ignorant than young school children. The strangest thing of all about them is that they refuse to take any form of refreshment – even European food.

"We would like to know how this mystery aligns itself with any similar experiences in the United States. Frankly, we are not a little afraid of the possible consequences in the light of Mr. Gray Barker's disturbing book.

"I do not want you to reproduce any of the material which I have enclosed. These phrases have been chosen from six letters that I have seen for myself. The recipients are particularly anxious not to be identified and they realize this would be possible if the 'International Bankers' had an opportunity to compare the individual phraseologies with the copies that it is feared that they may make of their strange correspondence."

NOORALI KASSAMALI KANJI

Bombay, India

Others have received letters from this international silence group. George Adamski reported in "Flying Saucers Farewell" that he was jeered by a group of these persons while giving a lecture regarding space people. They even went so far as to start a riot, which brought in the police.

Where this sinister group of men comes from is still not too clear, but the answer is bound to come to light sometime in the future.

UFOLOGY'S PAST RESEARCHER

In early February of 1962, Bill Boyer (formerly Bill Ashbay) received a most unusual postcard from Lisle, Illinois. It is reproduced below for those of you who have not read it before.

"Dear Bill,

Just received letter from T.G Beckley regards membership in your organization, and the first thing that hit me was – when the truth of the matter is discovered – what then??? (You can't print it.) Those that have found it have completely disappeared from the face of the Earth. (I know – I happen to be one of the fortunate ones who found it. And am also fortunate to yet remain.

Sincerely,

A Past Researcher."

> Dear Bill: Just received letter from T.G. Beckley regards membership in your organization; an the first thing that hit me was — when the _truth_ of the _matter_ is discovered — What then??? — (you can't print it.) Those that have found it — have — completely disappeared from the face of the Earth. (I know) — I happen to be one of the fortunate ones, who found it. And am also fortunate, to yet, remain. Sincerely
> A Past researcher

This person, whose name and address are known to me, was carrying out an investigation into a certain type of coil winding necessary to produce a composite wave form that could be used with an infrared transmitter and receiver for communication with UFOs. This type of wave form is used to convert celestial light bodies into sound.

Other attempts to contact UFOs have proven successful. Mr. J. Cookes of Cheshire, England, claims to have a strange communications device whereby he has contacted space people.

A Mr. Van den Berg of Natal, South Africa, claims he has some sort of code with which he can indirectly communicate with these beings.

It seems from reading Albert Bender's book, **"Flying Saucers and the Three Men,"** that Mr. Bender was also trying to contact these unearthly visitors. When this proved to be successful, further attempts were made.

TWELVE MONTHS OF TERROR IN THE SKY

When the information sheet regarding this volume was released, I was asked why I stated that more angel hair than ever before had fallen from the sky. The reason is quite simple.

Many instances describing falls from the sky of such substances as angel hair, rocks, ice and animal matter have been reported during the last year. So far the number received by INS alone has been 24 for the period indicated. Since most of these have been detailed in our other publications, there is little need to reprint them here.

However, just to mention a few: Angel hair in Hialena, Florida, and Salt Lake City, Utah; four months of rock falls in Big Bear, California, and many similar reports.

During the summer months a total of 19 plane crashes took place, killing 90 percent of the passengers onboard at the time. During one month, eight different crashes took place. So it looks like something besides saucers comes in flaps.

Air Traffic Control stated that for the majority of the cases no answer had been found and that further investigations and research were being carried on. Any more information could only be gotten from news media, it was added.

In most sky falls, UFOs are in the area at the time. This is evidenced by the many Salt Lake City and Big Bear, California, reports at the time the angel hair and rocks were falling. It is difficult to understand just what this material is used for. This is just one of the mysteries we shall have to solve in due time. Or perhaps it is the intention of these interplanetary craft to use these items for hostility. A force field that surrounds these objects has in the past given a number of pilots trouble. This force field, which apparently can be turned off and on, seems to be the cause of cars stopping and is certainly the cause of a number of deaths.

The problem concerning this field of power is an important one, for it seems all these craft do not have such a field. These I am applying to Earth-made (German, in this case) machines. Perhaps the power which creates this field cannot be duplicated on this Earth. Only time and future research will tell.

DID SOVIET SPACEMEN DIE IN SPACE?

Western space authorities have said they know several Soviet cosmonauts have died for their country in space.

The following data were compiled from civilian space authorities in non-communist nations where tracking stations are operated.

If any of you reading this know of any other cases, we wish that you would make them public. We are grateful to *"FATE Magazine,"* which covered the first full story, written by Frank Edwards.

CASE #1: In February, 1959, Soviet cosmonaut Terentlu Shiborin, an Air Force officer, was launched into space at Kapustan Yar near the Black Sea. He radioed back for 28 minutes, then mysteriously stopped. Nothing was heard of him again.

CASE #2: On October 11, 1960, Col. Piotr Ivanovitch Dolgov was placed into orbit. Broadcasts of his mission were monitored for 30 minutes; then contact was broken. His name, prominent as holder of several records in parachute jumping, was never mentioned again in connection with his flight. More than two years later, this past November, "Red Star," the central organ of the Soviet Defense Ministry, announced the accidental death while fulfilling his duties, without giving any details.

CASE #3: On November 20, 1969, signals from an unidentified Soviet cosmonaut, sending the frantic message, "World, SOS – SOS" were monitored briefly, then faded.

CASE #4: On February 2, 1961, another unidentified Soviet cosmonaut was placed into orbit. Western tracking stations registered his breathing and heartbeat for a half-hour; then there was silence.

CASE #5: Cosmonaut Vassilyevitch Zovodovsky was launched on April 7, 1961, a few days before his successful compatriot, Gagarin. His contact with the ground was lost seconds after blastoff.

CASE #6: On May 17, 1961, two cosmonauts, a male and a female, were launched together in one capsule from Baikonur, near the Aral Sea. Tracking stations in Canada, Hawaii, in Bochum (West Germany), Jodrell Bank (England), Meudon (France), Uppsala (Sweden) and Turin (Italy) intercepted and recorded their conversation. It was not possible to ascertain their names. Here is a word-for-word transcript of the recording:

"While we are studying the program, the situation becomes critical for us. Something went wrong. We are changing our course. I am talking with the director. Do you understand? If we do not get out, the world will never learn about it anyway. You will know what to do. What? What? Here! Here there is something! There is something!"

These were the last words heard. Contact was lost at 8 P.M. local Moscow time.

CASE #7: On September 30, 1961, the Soviet newspaper Pravda surprisingly predicted a manned mission to the moon. A few days later, on October 14, 1961, the tracking station near Turin (Torre Bert tracking station) recorded clearly the voices of a man and a woman again in a single spacecraft. For seven hours, their conversation was heard by all the above mentioned tracking stations and by stations in Dakar (Senegal), Tokyo, and Sydney. After this long period of time, all contact was lost.

The U.S. National Aeronautics and Space Administration was contacted for confirmation in all the above cases. A spokesman, following NASA's security policy, indicated he could neither confirm nor deny the report as it then stood.

TRACES OF RETOUCHING FOUND ON RUSSIAN MOON PHOTO

Copies of the Soviet photo showing the dark side of the moon taken by a lunar probe (Lunik) in October, 1959, were distributed throughout the entire world. These photos have apparently been retouched, a leading Japanese astronomer averred.

If you can recall, the Lunik was launched on October 4, 1959, and the photo was taken three days later, on October 7, and shown to the world much later, on October 26. Dr. Shataro Miyamote, director of the Kazan Astronomical Observatory, a branch of Kyoto University, said he reached the conclusion that the Soviet moon photo is inaccurate in some respects, due to careless retouching. He has sent a full report to the International Astronomical Union's planetary committee meeting, and it is to be reviewed this July.

Dr. Miyamote, carrying out observations of the moon's circumference with a Cook reflecting telescope installed at the Kyoto observatory, noticed in March of 1962 that a portion of the far side of the moon was visible when the moon inclined some eight degrees. His staff succeeded in taking clear pictures of that part of the moon twice, on March 10 and 11.

Comparing his with the Soviet moon picture, he found that the two did not look totally alike. Especially surprising to the professor was that the Mare and Smith Sea on the western side of the moon, which he confirmed in his calculations, were totally smeared out in the Soviet picture.

Even before Dr. Miyamote, scientists from the United States' NASA had raised a question about the authenticity of the Soviet prints, and a scientist at the RAND Corporation in Los Angeles was first to discover a certain amount of retouching after it was enlarged several hundred times.

In Arizona, Professor Gerald Kuiper, who is director of the Armagh Astronomical Observatory, also has expressed growing doubts about this unearthly photo.

Other important scientists throughout the Free World also doubt the photo's veracity.

An article was published in one of the leading "dirt" magazines a few months after the story was given to the press. At the time, it was laughed at, but there is no laughing anymore. The question now is why.

SECRET SATELLITES OF THE U.S. AIR FORCE

While the debate regarding the Russian photos of the back side of the moon went on, a perhaps even stranger mystery was taking place – that of the mysterious satellites which the Air Force was sending up almost every other week into polar orbits.

The first such secret satellite was placed into orbit on November 22, 1961. A further list of these satellites is presented below. Unfortunately, it is not complete.

1961

1. Samos/Midas? Sent into orbit on November 22. No details released.

2. Samos/Midas? Sent into orbit on December 22. No details released.

1962

1. Discoverer? No orbit achieved. January 13.

2. Discoverer? February 21. No data released.

3. Midas 5. April 9. No further data released.

4. Discoverer? April 18. No further data released.

5. Discoverer? March 29? No further data released.

6. July 19. Believed to be top secret Midas. Released from Point Arguello, California. No further data.

7. Midas? August 12? No further data.

8. October 1. No further data.

Mum was the word on these shots, so much so that what few details were given never reached the press for lack of interest. Thus, the above information may be slightly incorrect and is not complete by any means.

Why are these satellites being sent up? Read further as we piece together these important parts of the puzzle.

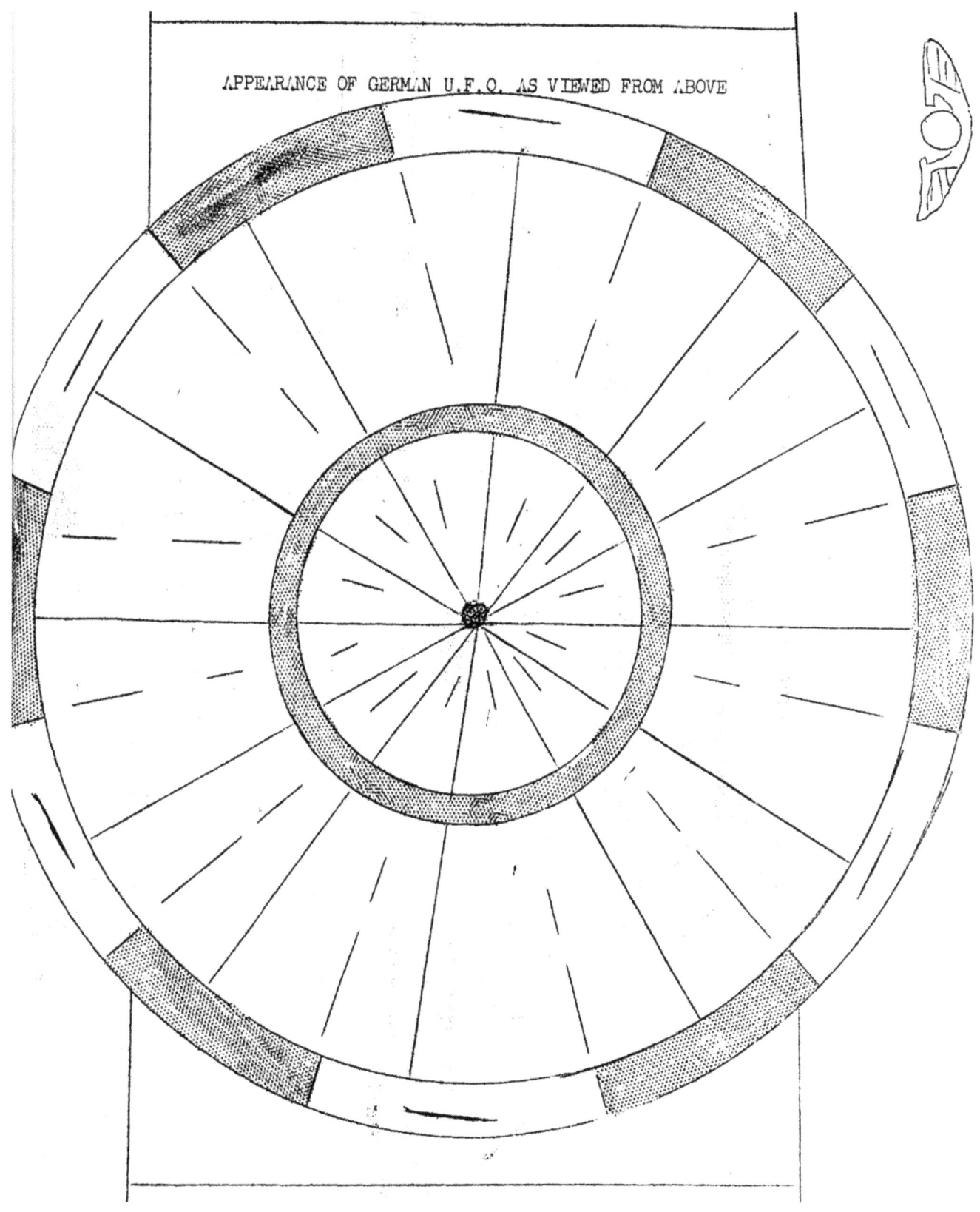

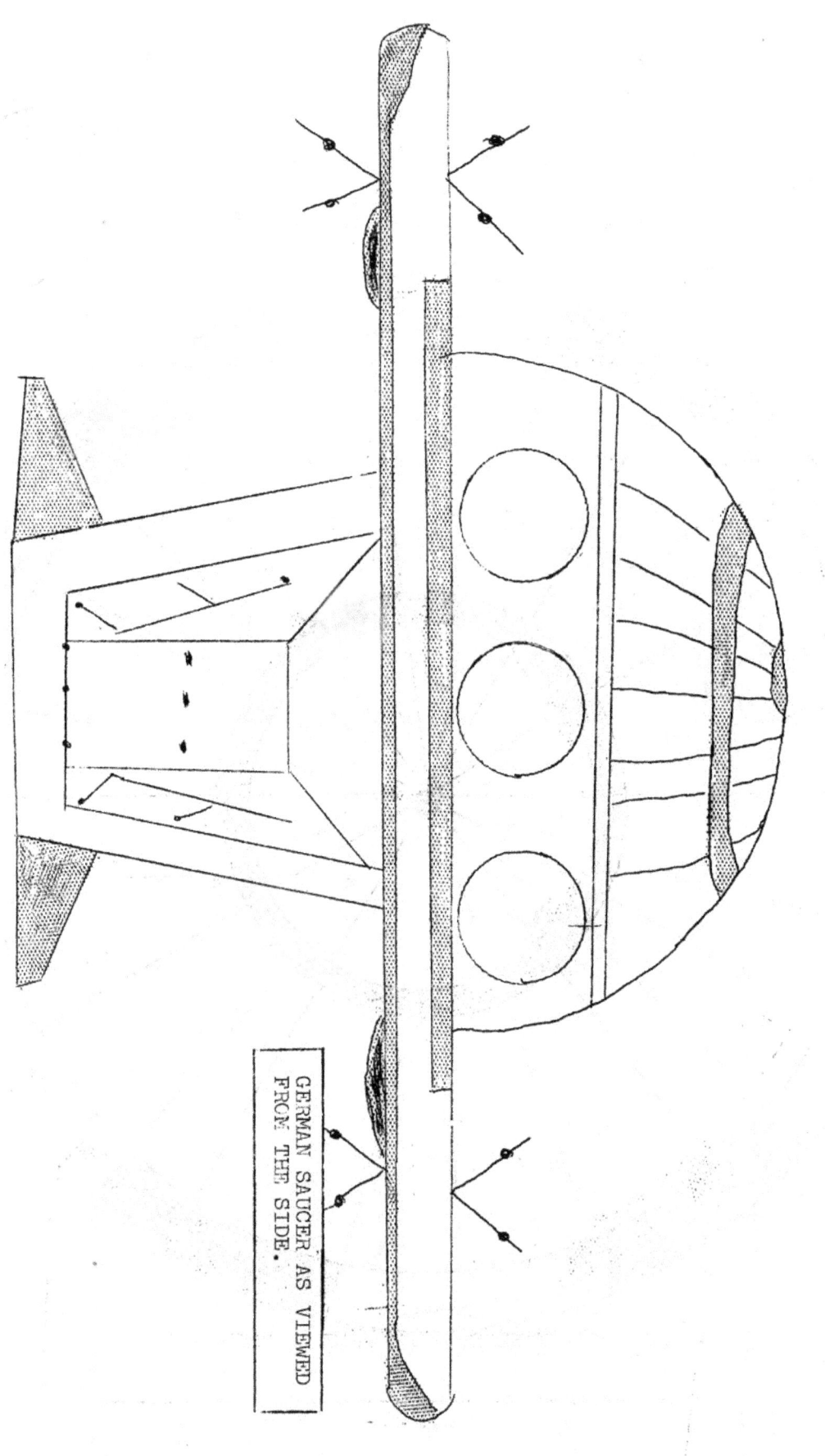

GERMAN SAUCER AS VIEWED FROM THE SIDE.

THE BENDER MYSTERY AND THE ANSWER TO THE FLYING SAUCER RIDDLE

By Timothy Green Beckley and Jerome Clark

THE SILENCING

IN mid-1952 a Bridgeport, Connecticut, man named Albert K. Bender organized a UFO research group which he called the International Flying Saucer Bureau. The IFSB was well-received, and by the next year it had grown to become the largest such organization in the world, with representatives in most states as well as in several foreign countries. Branch groups had been set up in England and France, and there was every reason for believing the IFSB would not be short-lived.

However, with the publication of the fifth issue of the organization's magazine, "*Space Review*," Bender announced the termination of the IFSB, giving no reason for doing so. On the first page of the issue (dated October, 1953), though, were several odd statements describing a "reliable source" which "has informed us that the investigation of the flying saucer mystery and solution is approaching its final stages.

"This same source, to whom we had referred data which has come into our possession, suggested that it was not the proper method and time to publish this data in '*Space Review*.'"

Another first page item, headed "Statement of Importance," read, "The mystery of the flying saucers is no longer a mystery. The source is already known, but any information about this is being withheld by orders from a higher source. We would like to print the full story in '*Space Review*,' but because of the nature of the information we are sorry that we have been advised in the negative.

"We advise those engaged in saucer work to please be very cautious."

Exactly what had caused Bender to write these peculiar comments was not widely known for some time. Shortly before the October issue was released, however, he informed several close associates (namely August C. Roberts, Dominic C. Lucchesi, and Gray Barker) that three men in black suits had paid him a visit in which they told him the answer to the saucer mystery. The solution, it was claimed, so upset Bender that he had been unable to hold food down for three days.

Albert K. Bender

The exact date of the visit has never been ascertained, but it seems to have taken place sometime between September 9 and 16. Gray Barker, who later chronicled in detail what has become known as the "Bender Mystery" (see ***They Knew Too Much About Flying Saucers***," University Books, 1956) calls attention to two letters he received from the Bridgeport researcher, one dated the 9th and the other the 16th. The first letter was penned in Bender's usual style, but the second "didn't sound right. It was formal, stilted, not like Bender at all. Since we had become very good friends through the mail, our letters were quite informal and contained many references of a personal nature. This one sounded odd, if only because of its abrupt, businesslike manner." Moreover, about that time Roberts spoke to Bender in a classic telephone conversation in which the latter told for the first time the story of the three men.

We shall probably never know the complete circumstances surrounding the visitation, but from the little Bender revealed at the time, we can state the following with a reasonable amount of certainty: Bender had been thinking of a UFO theory, which he eventually sent to a certain other person. Shortly thereafter the three men came, and one of them was carrying in his hand the same sheet of paper that Bender had mailed. The visitors were very threatening in their manner, hinting at dire consequences if Bender printed his theory, as he had originally intended to do. For several hours two of the men drilled the researcher on the explanation for the UFO mystery, while the third merely sat and carefully observed Bender. The story they gave was "fantastic" and extremely frightening, Bender later said, and it portended great changes in all fields of human endeavor, particularly in science. The United States government had known what the saucers are for "two years" (since 1951); it would release the answer in either five months (February 1954) or in "about four years" (1957).

When asked what would happen if he were to release the information he had been given, Bender stated, "I would likely go down in history. Also, I would go to jail for quite a long time."

Perhaps the oddest action of the three men was their confiscating Bender's file of back issues of "*Space Review,*" even though they had already been released and were in wide circulation.

Their final action was the editing of the October issue of the magazine, which had as yet to be released. Just before they left, one of them stopped by the door and said, "In our government we have the smartest men in the country. They can't find a defense for it. How can YOU do anything about it?" He added, "I suppose you know you're on your honor as an American. If I hear another word from your office, you're in trouble."

A short time later Bender received another visit; this time, however, by only one of the men. Ostensibly the knowledge imparted the second time served to lessen the harshness of that revealed earlier, for Bender felt "much better" afterward.

The last contact Bender had with mysterious silencers was a telephone call received after he made "a bad slip" in a long distance conversation with another UFO researcher. The call came from Washington, D.C., and a threatening voice warned Bender to be more careful in the future.

From this point on, Bender refused to discuss anything else concerned with the three men and what he had been told regarding the saucer mystery. He maintained a complete silence on the subject, despite mounting pressure brought on by the publication of Gray Barker's book in 1956. Finally, however, the next year he consented to write a short article which appeared in the November, 1957, issue of *Flying Saucers From Other Worlds.* In it Bender contradicted his earlier advice to investigators (that it was useless to pursue the UFO problem any further), stating: "My advice to all researchers is not to give up your search for the answers to the UFO enigma and to have faith in what you are doing. Be calm and composed about the whole thing until a day arrives when we will all know the answer, cruel as it will be."

Bender again lapsed into silence, until 1962, when he announced he was ready to tell all he knew.

THE ANSWER

If the above details are familiar to those readers who have studied the Bender Mystery, we apologize. But at the same time we find it necessary to include them in order to understand better their relationship to Bender's "explanation" as detailed in his recent book, ***Flying Saucers and the Three Men***" (Saucerian, 1962).

Basing our conclusions upon the information given by Bender prior to the publication of his work, we are led irrevocably to the conclusion that the three men were agents of the United States government – reference the mention of "our country" and their final admonition that Bender was on his honor "as an American" not to tell what he knew. There is also the matter of the telephone call from Washington, indicating that his phone was tapped by government representatives.

Several serious objections to this theory are immediately apparent, however. First, it is unlikely in the extreme that these agents would so distinguish themselves by their unique apparel and, second, that they would act in such a threatening manner, contrary to the methods used by American law officers.

There is also a rather puzzling detail to which, so far as we know, no one has called attention. In the last "*Space Review*" Bender mentions a source to which he had referred UFO information. "This same source suggested that it was not the proper method and time to publish it in '*Space Review*.'" Elsewhere, in an interview with Roberts and Lucchesi, Bender described how the visit had come about: "I was turning a theory over and over in my mind. When I got some actual names and places to back it up, I submitted it to someone. Then the men came." Was this "someone" one of the three men? It was Bender's visitors who "suggested that it was not the proper method and time to publish" his theory and the "same source" expressed identical sentiments. Bender nowhere states that the "source" was one of his visitors, but neither does he deny it. To the contrary, he seems strongly to imply it.

From the original account we arrive at the following conclusions about the three men and their visit:

INSIDE THE SAUCERS - MR. UFOS TEENAGE YEARS

1. The men wore black suits and were normal in appearance.

2. They arrived at Bender's home by conventional means.

3. Their information was imparted via drill-lecture.

4. Bender at all times remained in his own home during the visit.

Last year Bender authored his now famous "Flying **Saucers and the Three Men**," in which he dealt in great detail on his silencing and how it came about. It is hardly worth describing the whole series of alleged happenings, for many readers are undoubtedly familiar with the book's contents. The major points are summarized: Preceding the closing of IFSB, Bender had a number of odd experiences of the poltergeist variety, during most of which a sulfur-like odor was prevalent. Several times he received mysterious phone calls warning him to discontinue his research into matters that did not concern him, and finally three black-suited creatures with glowing eyes appeared out of nowhere (whether by astral projection or teleportation is not made clear); Bender was taken to a saucer base in Antarctica, where he learned that the UFOs were spacecraft from a planet, Kazik (pronounced KAY-ik), from a solar system light years away.

In appearance, the occupants resembled the famous "Flatwoods monster," and their purpose was the gleaning of certain chemicals from the ocean, a side effect of which was the creation of angel hair, Bender claims. However, refined methods, developed in 1952, stopped such falls. The beings were uninterested in human problems and for the most part abstained from contact. They arrived in 1945, says Bender, and departed 15 years later.

Under other circumstances, UFO researchers, having read the fantastic account, would shrug and write the whole Bender affair off as a hoax. Unfortunately, this cannot be done, for to do so leaves numerous questions unanswered. For example, even such critics as James W. Moseley have admitted that Bender is obviously sincere. Writes the "*Saucer News*" editor: "I was amazed, upon talking with Bender, to find him such a pleasant fellow who was obviously sincere about his story. This amazement was intensified when I sat down at the WOR microphones with Barker, him and Long John Nebel, and heard his story as it went out over the air. Frankly, I was ready to really 'give it to Bender,' but his complete sincerity, however, left me rather flabbergasted. I found myself listening, with some fascination, to his account, rather than trying to 'cut him up.' I think that Long John was similarly impressed."

We also beg the question if we accept Bender's story, for it contradicts almost everything previously known about the silencing. To point out but a few of the many absurdities and unanswered puzzles:

1. There is no mention of the "certain source" to whom Bender sent his theory nor that he ever suggested such a theory.

2. No explanation is given for the supposedly "fantastic" and "frightening" nature of the flying saucer mystery's solution. (To some persons, the interstellar solution advanced by Bender would be considered both "fantastic" and "frightening." But, as that theory is and was widely accepted by UFOlogists, it would probably not be so to Bender, who was also a science fiction fan.)

3. Bender does not attempt to explain such silencings as those of Laimon Mitris (called "Gordon Smallwood" in Barker's 1956 book) or Edgar Jerrold, which, though apparently related to Bender's, describe completely terrestrial agents. (At the time of the silencings, Jerrold, Bender, and New Zealander Harold Fulton were working on "Project X," apparently connected with a possible saucer base in Antarctica. Fulton was not silenced, but he did report some weird occurrences which he believed were connected with his saucer investigation.

4. The two most glaring errors are his claims about angel hair and the span of saucer visitation. First, the vast majority of angel hair cases have occurred SINCE 1952, and, second, it is obvious UFOs have not left us, as can be determined by reading the first two sections of this book.

5. Most reports of UFOs entering and leaving the oceans were chronicled long BEFORE 1945.

Contrasting Bender's original story with his later one, we are led to the inevitable conclusion that the first is accurate but the second is not. How, then, do we explain his apparent sincerity?

The most likely explanation is that Bender was subjected to some kind of hypnosis, making him believe a false and ridiculous account so as to lead researchers astray. Indicative of this is peculiar word "Kazik" (KAY-ik), supposedly the name of the planet from which the extraterrestrials originated. Nowhere is there any record of Bender's seeing this word in print, and so the only logical conclusion is that he would spell it phonetically. One gets the impression that Bender got the name from a script which he memorized.

Who ARE the men in black, and what is their purpose? We do not know. We may never know. Some guesses on this subject, though, are given below.

INS CHIEF OF INVESTIGATION .... James C. Kelsey

About Bender, ha. I'm not quite sure where the saucers come from, maybe straight from Bender's mind! Bender's story must be weighed against the reports after 1960, since Bender says they left then. But even if there are irrefutable sightings, Bender can say that he was told a false story by the entities.

INS ASSISTANT EDITOR .... Jerome Clark

It is my personal belief that some kind of organized resistance to flying saucer research does exist and that this resistance not only comes from the government, but from some other source – and this is where the "men in black" come in. Bender's recent story is obviously not correct; it is probable that Bender was forced to write the book, invent a ridiculous story, and thus make researchers tend to ignore the whole enigma. I think I have a pretty good idea as to who these "silencers" are, but I prefer to do more investigation before discussing my findings.

I also feel that these forces, or agents of them, have penetrated into the UFO field, that they keep careful watch on those interested in the subject. However, I doubt if Lonzo Dove, Jim Moseley, Karl Hunrath, or any of the others sometimes accused of being agents of this "silence group" really are. It would seem more logical that these individuals would tend to shy away from controversy and that they would do everything to keep their association from even being suspected.

It is not impossible; moreover, that much of the confusion existing in modern UFOlogy is organized. Coral Lorenzen, writing in a recent APRO Bulletin, makes the fascinating suggestion that some of the contact claimants actually believe they have encountered benevolent space people, when in truth these UFO beings may have quite different purposes: to make people believe they are friendly when in actuality they are hostile. You may have noticed when reading accounts by "contactees" that almost invariably the claimants are rather naïve, gullible people to start with; more hardheaded persons would suspect something when space people ramble on about their good intentions but do nothing to carry them out.

INS SECRETARY .... Dale N. Rettig

I view the Bender book with mixed emotions. I would like to believe Bender, and, had he written it in 1954, I would believe him completely. An interesting theory is that he wrote the book to hide the real truth, which could be more fantastic than what is in the book. Personally, I do not believe this theory, though. Let's say I believe him in a number of areas, while I remain doubtful in others.

INS ADVISORY BOARD MEMBER .... James W. Moseley

In regard to Bender, all I can tell you is that he is a very likable person, but I do not believe his story at all, and I doubt if more than a very few people do. It is too fantastic to be believable. I still say that Bender is behind the whole thing, in his usual money-grabbing way. You are correct in saying that the saucers, whatever they are, did not leave in 1960. On the Long John Show I made a point of asking Bender about this. I pointed out also that, although newspaper coverage of sightings may be dying off a bit, the Air Force received more sightings in 1960 and 1961 than in 1959. In other words, there was a slight increase over 1959, which was a more or less average year. Bender had no real answer regarding any of these objections I raised.

INS ENGLAND MEMBER .... Peter Bexon

I have a theory about the Bender book that it is: 1.) true. 2.), if not, the book has been written by Bender to put investigators off the track of the real solution to the saucer mystery (possibly under orders from the "three men"). 3.) I am convinced that Bender has not perpetrated a hoax for monetary gain. In fact, I am convinced that the "men in black" exist and were NOT invented by Bender or anyone else. 4.) There is also a possibility that the three men did not tell Bender the truth but a false story invented to fit the facts as Bender knew them.

DIRECTOR FLYING SAUCER RESEARCH ORGANIZATION............Robert Mastroberte

In simple, down-to-earth terms, the Bender book is great.

The below opinion is from a saucer researcher from New York City, well-known in the field, who does not want his name mentioned but wishes that the following be published so that all concerned may read it:

Regarding Moseley, I am beginning to suspect that there's more than meets the eye to him. Recalling our recent phone conversation, you asserted that you had felt that Jim and Gray's feud may have been the result of their conspiring to push their periodicals. While I had never denied this possibility, the more I considered, the more ludicrous it appeared to be. First of all, Barker publishes '*Saucerian Bulletin*' very rarely, so any publicity that may be obtained through a phony feud would immediately be offset by this very fact. Moreover, Moseley has been obtaining publicity through his many recent appearances on the Long John program. Surely any publicity he might obtain through Barker would be at a minimum.

Secondly, it might be very apropos to consider Moseley's latest claim to fame: a visit to Wright-Patterson Air Force Base, the home of Project Blue Book. It appears to me that since this visit, Jim has been repeating the Air Force party line more than ever. In fact, he used to distribute their notorious fact sheets to his readership. The question arises as to why. Why should he continue to expound their gobbledygook? Why, when the Air Force disavowed Tacker's book, did Jim suddenly come out with an unfavorable review of same? Why does Moseley continually visit the Pentagon year after year to contact the Public Information Officer? To obtain orders, or what?

Now, in view of Barker's releasing of the Bender book "***Flying Saucers and the Three Men***," Moseley is trying to discredit his veracity by accusing him of drinking or implying that Gray is in need of a ghostwriter and both. At first I thought it humorous that Moseley made this rather flimsy accusation. Now it appears that his intent was to establish a record of incompetence for Barker. As you recall, the Bender book is allegedly presenting inside information about the mysterious Silence Group, their activities and a possible solution to the saucer enigma. Wouldn't an Air Force agent of some sort want to somehow prevent publication of this book, by scaring the persons involved, by discrediting their integrity? Is Moseley part of one of their carefully laid plans?

Now let us consider more info. For the past five years, Jim has issued vehement denunciations of NICAP. In the September, 1959, issue of his "*Saucer News*," one of his staff members endeavored to tear apart the Major's third book, "***The Flying Saucer Conspiracy***," which, as you recall, presented inside information regarding the Silence Group. Even when Major Keyhoe proved the obvious erroneous nature of the allegations, Moseley maintained his irrational position, even in the face of a possible lawsuit. Why?

In the June, 1959, issue of "Saucer News," Moseley's friend, Lonzo Dove, apparently under prompting by Jim, viciously censored Barker, even passing the remark that Barker was in actuality one of the men in black, or possibly the person who sent the authorities after Bender. Again, in the face of a possible lawsuit, Moseley continued to defend his position. Did he fear that Barker would somehow convince Bender to talk? Is he, de facto, somehow promoting the Air Force, and utilizing the pages of his saucer zine to discredit persons who are apparently doing SOMETHING to expose the Air Force conspiracy of silence?

Strange how I never actually considered the evidence which had accumulated until now! Possibly I would have discovered this paradox earlier, but suffice it to say I have finally put some pieces in the UFO jigsaw puzzle together.

And now let us look at the Barker record and recall some of the statements made about him by independent researchers. In 1957, when Palmer was first considering the publication of his then known "*Flying Saucers From Other Worlds*," CSI, a now inactive group, which had always cynically chastised all personages bearing even the vaguest relation to the contact-fringe, or having even a partially shady character, applauded the acquisition of Barker to the Palmer magazine, even though it expressed apprehensions (later confirmed) regarding the publication itself.

The more we evaluate the mounting evidence, the more we have to attest to Barker's veracity, and the more we have to discredit Moseley. I still consider Jim to be a nice guy, but his cannot detract from his shady record in UFO research.

The above mentioned details are not those of this researcher, and he would have appreciated it if the burden had not been laid on him for printing it in the first place. Since a copy of this book is being sent to Jim, he will have his chance to make any needed comment.

A mystery is about to be solved. We are beginning to think that Bender was tricked into believing that the German craft were interplanetary and put under hypnosis in order to make him believe the things he would not under normal conditions. The same goes for most of the other contactees. The biggest hoax comes from Reinhold Schmidt, who, according to C.A. Honey, George Adamski's business manager, saw in actuality a craft forced down by real space people. It was built, says Mr. Honey, by German scientists who were brought over after the War. When they saw Schmidt had observed their craft, they decided to make him think it was a spaceship in an effort to keep him from disclosing information (secret) that would be believed.

A few things are wrong with that theory. There is no proof that these German scientists whom he reportedly met were working for the government, but more likely they were working on their own. Further contacts with these "space people" were made, as in most cases, under hypnosis.

By this time the U.S. as well as the Russian government must be getting an inkling of what is flying through the sky. Thus, they have set up their own office to deal with the mystery. The Central Intelligence Agency has given the Air Force orders to say nothing about them so that the public will have no idea of what is going on until the whole mystery is solved. Therefore, the Air Force sent up secret satellites into polar orbits, the same places where Bender claimed to have visited saucer bases. These satellites are perhaps taking photos of the area in the hope of coming up with something of great importance.

The reason for the retouching of the moon photos by the Russians now becomes clear. There are two possible answers. 1.) The Germans have settled on the far side, where under normal conditions they cannot be observed. When the Soviet leaders saw the shots, they weren't shocked – it just proved their theory regarding the UFOs was correct. 2.) Perhaps some interplanetary race has built a settlement on the moon, and the threat of an unknown evil force was too much to be given to the public all at once.

The UFO mystery is drawing to a timely end. Perhaps the upcoming two or three years will tell us for certain just who is right and just who is wrong. The information in this volume is not hearsay, nor is it presented as a final answer, but as merely the findings of one researcher who has spent all his spare time, plus endless amounts of money, on a subject that interests him greatly. It began as a hobby but has branched out into something more important than that. It is a way of life, of which I am proud. If I am a crackpot, then I have good company: Dr. Oberth, Prof. Maney, Dr. Fontes, General

MacArthur, Admiral Hillenkoetter, Frank Edwards, Prof. Tombaugh, astronaut Gordon Cooper, and countless others. If we are all nuts, pity the world.

If it, however, turns out that the saucers, indeed, exist, as we know for certain they do, then there is a great possibility that there are more crackpots in scientific circles than there are in UFOlogy. Perhaps, as Jerome Clark once said to me, the real crackpots are those who, despite piles of evidence to the contrary, believe that something does not exist merely because it does not happen to agree with their theories.

Perhaps a word to the wise would be the best way to close this section off: to believe is one thing, but to prove is another. Who is telling the truth? Who means what he says? Who really knows? We have the "lunatic fringe" to deal with. But then who can really and truthfully say which person is a lunatic? Certainly not because of one's ideas! This is one of the beliefs of the Interplanetary News Service, that everyone should have his say. Let's prove, think, and, most importantly, ACT in the years to come. It will make easier the finding of the answer for which we have all been searching. The question, of course: ARE BEINGS FROM OTHER PLANETS WATCHING THE EARTH? FOR WHAT REASON? The German weapon idea is not enough. There is more, and with your help all can be solved in the near future.

CURRENT UFO SHOTS
CAPTIONS AND EXPLANATIONS FOR PHOTOS

1. George D. Fawcett, well-known lecturer and writer on the subject of flying saucers. He is currently serving on the board of advisors of the Interplanetary News Service, and his article can be found elsewhere in this volume. His illustrated lectures have been well received by over 85 groups and organizations in the United States and Panama.

2. On Monday, April 23, 1962, Homer Schaefer sighted and was able to photograph a UFO while in his backyard carrying on a hunt for several meteors. He decided to get his Polaroid land camera, which had a 3000-speed film, so that he could get a shot of a meteor for his collection. While waiting, he noticed a dark object cross the sky very slowly. He recognized it as a flying saucer, the same type that he had seen on previous occasions. It made a close approach to the city, at rooftop level, hovered over a street, then headed in a southerly direction. Schaefer described this craft as being approximately 50 feet in size, about 200 feet above the street, and several hundred yards from where he stood. It glided silently past at a speed of some 40 mph. The photo he took of it did not turn out satisfactorily, so he decided to watch again, hoping to get another shot. At 10:30 P.M., as he stood in the bitter cold of the Kitchener, Ontario, Canada, air facing west, the direction the UFO had taken, he was suddenly startled to see the sky above light up. Glancing up, he saw a huge UFO directly above him and managed to get another shot just as it passed over him. It was a much larger craft than the first one, with numerous lights around it and with a crescent shape. The weather at the time was clear. The object left no smoke or vapor trail, and appeared to be transparent. Mr. Schaefer believes that the UFO originated from Venus or possibly another dimension. He also thinks they were powered by an electromagnetic drive which affected his sensitive film, producing, thus, the transparent objects. Mr. Schaefer is a public school caretaker and is highly respected. Thanks go both to Gene Duplantier, who interviewed the witness, and Schaefer himself, who has since that day taken a great interest in the subject of UFOlogy.

3. The three weird figures shown in the third photo were found about five years ago in the Nevada desert. They were sent to the Anthropology Department at the University of Utah. The university has informed us that it remembers the figures but does not remember the story behind the objects. The photo shown was copied from the original photograph, which was made when the objects were first brought to Salt Lake City. The university's conclusion was that the figures are fakes, made

out of plastic. However, the man who brought them – who just happens to be the owner of a plastic firm – insisted that they're real.

4. In this fourth shot, we see Robert Miller (smoking) and Ricky Hilberg as they take part in the first of a series of nationwide UFO conference calls. Such personalities as George Popowitch, Jerome Clark, Alan Katz, Dale N. Rettig, Allen Greenfield, Harry Siebert, and yours truly have taken part in the hookup. They were started to discuss unity between the major flying saucer organizations now in operation. From these calls came plans for a public information sheet to be released by all the groups interested to the public, radio, TV and other news media in their area. These calls were jointly sponsored by IUY and the UUA.

5. This photograph shows Alex Birch and Walter Revill with the cameras that made them well-known in the field of UFOlogy. Both stories are detailed elsewhere in this book.

6. This picture was taken by Alex Birch over Mosbrough, Sheffield, England.

INSIDE THE SAUCERS - MR. UFOS TEENAGE YEARS

George D. Fawcett   1.

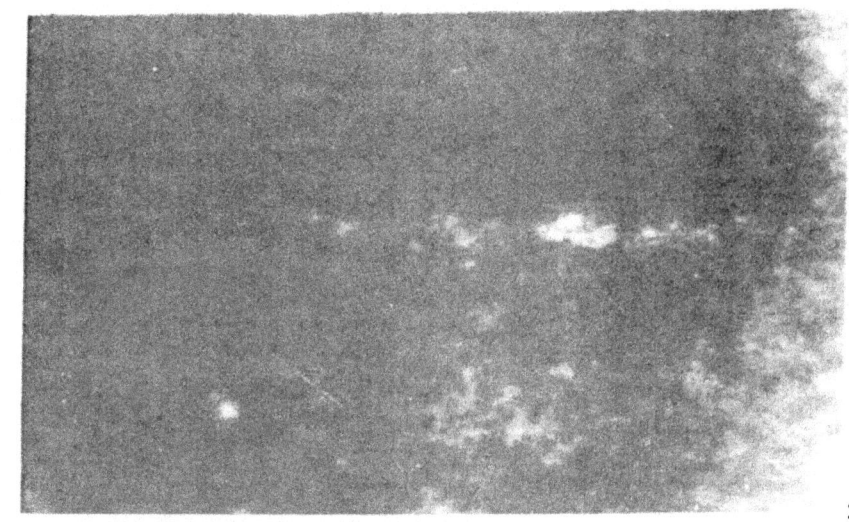

2.

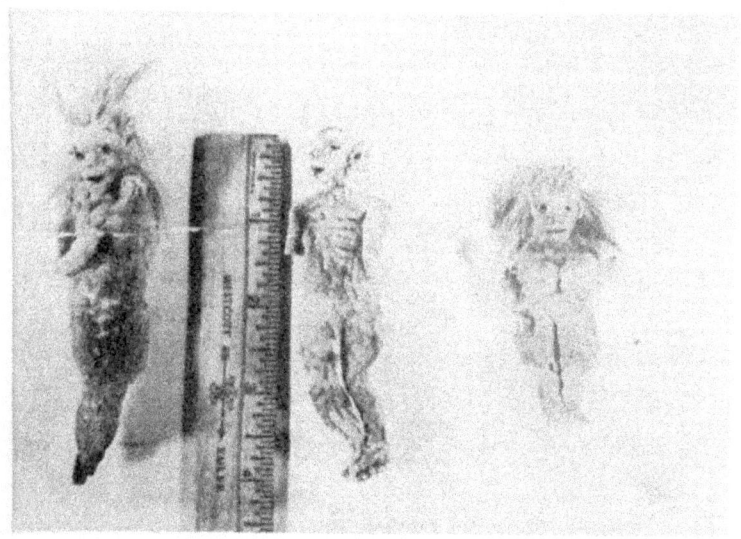

3.

4.

Young Alex Birch. With this box camera he snapped five dark "invaders" in the sky

Walter Revill. An eerie shape showed up as a vanishing point of light on his cine-film

Unidentified flying objects seen and photographed by Sheffield schoolboy Alex Birch on March 4 this year. Air Ministry experts' explanation: "Light refracted and reflected by ice particles in atmosphere."

5.   6.

THE UFO IN THE COFFER IN THE GREAT PYRAMID OF GIZA

By Kenneth L. Larson

FOR thousands of years of earth history, persons from various continents have pondered over the meaning of the Great Pyramid of Giza. This pyramid is located in Egypt and was evidently constructed around 2600 B.C. But archeologists are uncertain as to the name of the designer. It was built during the reign of the Pharaoh Cheops. Huge granite and limestone blocks of stone were utilized during the construction, and the blocks were fitted into place with a high degree of a accuracy and skill. Some of the blocks weighed 19 tons. The Great Pyramid is 481 feet high and has five sides and five corners.

Approximately 31 feet of stone is missing from the original apex. In looking at it from space, the pyramid has the shape of an X inside a square. It is oriented to the north, east, west and south points of the compass. The original entrance is located on the north side about fifty feet up from the base. The Great Pyramid is the only remaining wonder of the ancient Seven Wonders of the World.

After its construction, the Great Pyramid was evidently sealed and the original entrance hidden from sight. This entrance consisted of hinged blocks of stone. The pyramid had a white limestone casing of great brilliance in the desert sun. But this casing has been torn away and used for building blocks.

In about the 9th century A.D., the Arabs dug a hole into the side of the pyramid. While they were digging, a stone fell from within the pyramid and caused the discovery of the original entrance passage. This descending passage led down to a rough chamber below the level of the ground. About a third of the way down, a second passage slanted upward into a larger passage called the Grand Gallery. This second passage had been covered from sight by a stone inserted into the entrance. The Arabs discovered that a granite plug had been forced – or constructed – into the entrance of the second ascending passage. The tunnel diggers could not force the stone and had to dig around the site. After this obstacle, the diggers discovered that the Grand Gallery passage was filled with huge blocks of stone. As each block was broken up, another block would slide down into position.

After these huge, rectangular stones were removed, the diggers scrambled to the upper end of the Grand Gallery. At the upper end, they discovered a large stone block serving as a type of step 36 inches high. The men then entered a small chamber. Another low passage led from this into a larger one terms the King's Chamber. At the far west end of the chamber, a large, red, granite coffer rested on the floor. Expecting to find a mummy and a treasure in gold, the men rushed over to the coffer – and found it empty. The coffer did not contain a body nor have a lid. It was evidently larger in size than the plugged opening leading into the Grand Gallery. Certain writers think that the plug blocking the ascending passage was constructed into position (because of its peculiar shape), and, in a similar manner, the coffer was placed during the construction of the pyramid. If so, this would have prevented bringing either the coffer or a body into the King's Chamber – since the ascending passage had been blocked. (Marsham Adams referred to the King's Chamber as "The Chamber of the Open Tomb.") Influenced by early writers, John Taylor of London, England, published a book in 1859. He said that the designer of the Great Pyramid knew that the earth is a sphere. He came to the conclusion that the Great Pyramid was built in order to express the radius and diameter of a circle. He felt that the architect had embodied in the monument those dimensions which prove knowledge of the true size and shape of the earth. Professor Charles Piazzi-Smith, Astronomer Royal of Scotland, visited the Great Pyramid in 1865 and measured the internal and external features. He felt that the pyramid was the original model for all the pyramids. His measurements cited one side of the base as 9,131 inches. The four sides of the square base would total 36,524 pyramid inches. (He had come to the conclusion that the designer had utilized a system of measurement in which 1000 British inches would equal 999 pyramid inches.) The height of the pyramid was determined by him to be 5,813.01 pyramid inches. The 36,524 pyramid inches would represent the solar year of 365,242 days. The height (5,813.01) was converted to another number – with a resulting figure of 91,837,578. Piazzi-Smith felt that this figure represented the true distance from the earth to the sun.

The King's Chamber was 17 feet wide, 34 feet long, and 19 feet high. It was made from red granite blocks and engineered to a high degree of perfection. The floor of the chamber was even with the 50th level of the Great Pyramid. (There are about 201 existing levels.) The Queen's Chamber rested on the 25th level, and it was entered by a passage branching off from the ascending passage. The ascending passage sloped upward (Piazzi-Smith estimates) at 26 degrees. The King's and Queen's chambers were in line with the vertical apex of the pyramid. The entrance to the King's Chamber lay at the east end of the room. The length (34 feet) was double the width (17 feet), and the height (19 feet) was one-half the diagonal of the floor. The length of the chamber was equivalent to the diameter of a circle.

Professor Piazzi-Smyth estimated that the coffer was 90 inches long, 30 wide and 41 inches high. There were no inscriptions, and the lid has not been found. He said that the cubic contents of the coffer were equivalent to 71,214 cubic inches. The length plus the width was equal to 3.1415 (pi) times the height. Pi is the ratio of the diameter of a circle to its circumference.

The external measurements of the Great Pyramid (Piazzi-Smyth figures):

(1) Angle of apex: 76 degrees, 17'31.4"

(2) Angle of side: 51 degrees, 51'

(3) Angle of corner: 45 degrees and 90 degrees (plain view)

During the period of high noon, the sun would shine down on all five corners and four sides (the fifth side was the bottom). Piazzi-Smyth believes that the Great Pyramid was a mathematical, engineering, astronomical, geometrical and divine (prophetic) monument. He believes that the pyramid contained a mathematical and graphic record of the world and he referred to it as "a revelation in stone." To his mind, the Great Pyramid contained the same statements and prophecies as the Holy Bible.

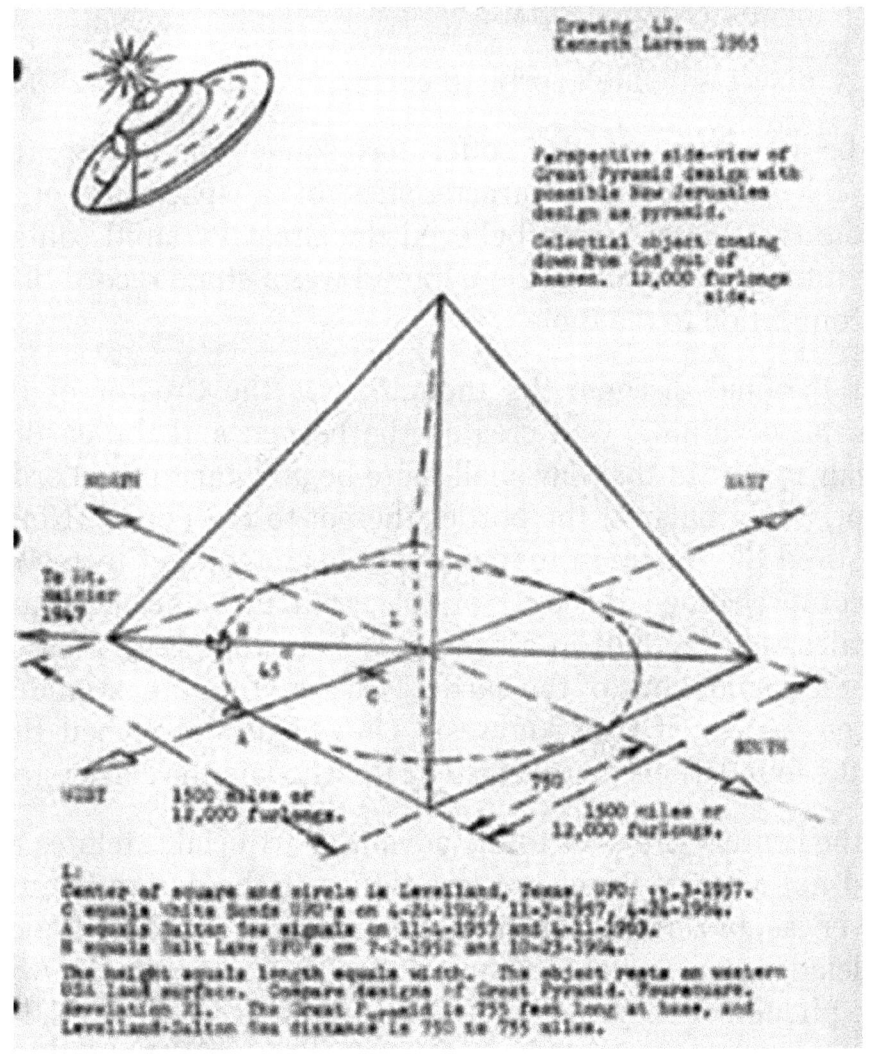

In the year 1957, the first artificial satellite was launched from the earth. The first American satellite was launched on January 31, 1958. A satellite travels at a certain velocity while in orbit around the earth. The velocity increases in orbits near the earth and decreases farther out from earth. At 100 miles, a satellite would last only a few days. With no atmosphere, a satellite could orbit at sea level. The first American satellite had an eccentric orbit (not a perfect circle) of about 300 miles altitude. At a height of 300 miles, the satellite would travel at 17,050 mph or 4.737 miles per second. At sea level, the velocity would be 17,830.8 mph or 4.953 mps. At 1075 miles, it would have a velocity of 15,700 mph. At 22,300 miles, the satellite would be stationary over one spot and would orbit once every 24 hours.

If the artificial satellite had an eccentric orbit, it could travel at 17,803.5 mph or 4.9454 mps. The figure of 17,803.5 was obtained in this manner:

1. 71.214 cubic inches in the coffer.

2. 71,214 divided by 4 (compass points): 17,803.5 cubic inches.

3. 17,803.5 inches: 17,803.5 mph.

4. 17,803.5: object/satellite in orbit of earth.

Could it be possible that the coffer has some relationship (as a measuring instrument) to the performance characteristics of a spaceship or satellite? It is interesting to note that Piazzi-Smyth believed the Great Pyramid contained records of the past and the future. To his mind, the pyramid was a stone record of the human race and had a close connection to the Bible.

The Great Pyramid designer, he thought, was the Creator of the earth. (Note Genesis 1:1, "In the beginning, God created the heaven and the earth." KJV.) Piazzi-Smyth cited Isaiah 19:19, "In that day shall there be an altar to the Lord in the midst of the land of Egypt, and a pillar at the border thereof to the Lord." (Note Isaiah 40:12z; "Who hath measured the waters in the hollow of his hand, and meted out heaven with the span, and comprehended the dust of the earth in a measure, and weighed the mountains in scales, and the hills in a balance?" Note Job 38:4, 5 and 6: "Where were you when I laid the foundations of the earth? Declare, if thou hast understanding. Who laid the measures thereof, if thou knowest? Or who has stretched the line upon it? Whereupon are the foundations thereof fasted? Or who laid the cornerstone thereof?)

Living in the century previous to the advent of artificial satellites and space flight, Piazzi-Smyth did not attempt to relate these things to the design features of the Great Pyramid. However, as an astronomer, he did discuss astronomical topics – such as the Pole Star, the Pleiades star cluster, the sun, the solar system, etc. He was evidently not familiar with the phenomenon of the UFO. On November 24, 1896, a UFO flew over San

Francisco, California, and was reported by dozens of citizens. It was seen a few minutes before 7:00 P.M. At about 7:00 P.M., a similar egg-shaped object flew over Red Bluff, California, at a high rate of speed. It was reported over Chico a few minutes after this. Red Bluff is 162 miles north of San Francisco and Chico is 42 miles southeast of Red Bluff.

Assuming that the same UFO appeared over all three cities, we could arrive at an approximate speed of 1944 mph. (Event reported in San Francisco and Oakland newspapers, November, 1896.)

On August 13, 1960, a UFO hovered over the ground 18 miles south of Red Bluff and in line with the position of San Francisco. According to the San Francisco Chronicle, August 17, 1960, the UFO flashed a red beam of light at two California State Patrolmen. The two officers beamed their red spotlight at the object hovering about 500 feet over the ground. The UFO then flew eastward, and the patrol car followed it for two hours. On August 14, 1960, similar UFOs were reported moving over Mineral – about 30 miles east of the August 13 event.

A UFO was sighted over Chico on July 17, 1960. In November, on the second and third, in 1957, seven different sightings of UFOs took place in an area centered on Levelland, Texas. The first UFO appeared on a highway four miles west of Levelland – egg-shaped and glowing a brilliant white. The second UFO appeared four miles east of Levelland. The third UFO was eight miles north, the fourth UFO was ten miles north, the fifth UFO was five miles west, the sixth UFO was three miles northwest and the seventh UFO was five miles northwest.

These reported sightings by patrolmen, citizens and police took place between 10:50 P.M., November 2, and 1:30 A.M., November 3, 1957. The objects were reported to have cut off car lights and radios. Similar objects were reported by two separate military patrols at the White Sands atomic test site – where the world's first atomic test took place on July 16, 1945. A UFO flashing a powerful light was reported near the Salton Sea, California, on November 4, 1957. (Source: *The Los Angeles Times*)

In July, 1952, and on August 13, 1952, numerous UFOs were sighted and observed on radar screens while performing over Washington, D.C. On June 24, 1947, nine UFOs were reported flying near Mount Rainier, Washington, by a private pilot named Kenneth Arnold. A UFO flashing a powerful beam of brilliant light hovered over Sistersville, West Virginia, on April 19, 1897. It was earlier reported over Chicago and Omaha, Nebraska. Other UFO reports come from France (1461 A.D.) and ancient Egyptian, Roman and British records.

The scope and breadth of the UFO makes it one of the most profoundly amazing problems mankind has ever encountered. Not the least amazing of its features is the fact that the reality and nature of the problem have gone unnoticed for so many centuries.

In March 1950 Commander McLaughlin, United States Navy, sighted and tracked a UFO with measuring instruments. This took place over the White Sands Proving Grounds, New Mexico. He estimated that the UFO had a velocity of 18,000 mph. The first rocket satellite was not launched until seven years later. The American rockets had a speed of about 18,000 mph, but this velocity was not reached until 1958.

For the sake of discussion, let us assume that the designer of the Great Pyramid of Giza embodied scientific and mathematical data into the pyramid. This design might have involved the performance characteristics and power capabilities of spaceships and artificial satellites. The designer would have known that at some stage or level of human history, the human race would uncover this evidence. The time of enlightenment would occur during the same time of development as space travel. This, of course, would imply the existence of a superior type of intelligence elsewhere in the universe – intelligences that had brought about or known of the original creation and design of the Planet Earth. These intelligences would serve the plans of the Creator of the Earth. The UFO would be related to the operations of these intelligences. At some time, the human race would enter into a higher level of intelligence and advanced life. The UFOs would seemingly be the forerunners of some unique and climactic event – all of the UFO reports would be preliminary operations pointing to a climactic moment and event.

What would this climactic event be? I think this climactic event involves the SECOND COMING OF JESUS CHRIST. Note Psalm 118:22: "The stone which the builders refused is become the headstone of the corner." Ephesians 2:20: "And are built upon the foundations of the apostles and prophets, Jesus Christ himself being the chief cornerstone." First Peter 2:6: "Wherefore also it is contained in the Scripture, 'Behold, I lay in Sion a chief cornerstone, elect, precious; and he that believes in him shall not be confounded.'"

Acts 4:11: "that by the name of Jesus Christ of Nazareth, this is the stone which was set at naught of your builders, which is become the head of the corner." St. Matthew 24:30: "And then shall appear the sign of the Son of Man in heaven; and then shall all of the tribes of earth mourn, and they shall see the Son of Man coming in the clouds of heaven with power and glory." Isaiah 63:2: "Wherefore art thou red in thine apparel, and thy garments like him that treads in the wine press?"

The UFO is a type of evidence or proof that a Creator designed the continents of the earth (in particular, the West Coast of the USA), as well as the Sun. The Great Pyramid of Giza embodies this mathematical design, formed by the Creator of all things.

In the past two and one-half years, much valuable, fruitful and amazing information has been made known to man. These data directly concern the Bible and the USA, making clear the reason for the founding of this nation in 1776, and the fact that this North American continent was formed according to an intelligent and mathematical design.

The UFO operations between 1947 and 1960 established these facts or acknowledged their awareness of these things:

1. Number of minutes in day: 1440.
2. Rotation velocity of earth: 1000 mph.
3. Number of days in solar year: 365.242.
4. Distance of sun to earth: 93,003,000 miles.
5. Diameter, radius and circumference of the earth.
6. Diameter, radius and circumference of the sun.
7. The Great Pyramid of Giza in Egypt.
8. Mount Sinai and Moses event.
9. Jerusalem. Bethlehem. Dead Sea Scrolls.
10. Design of the United States West Coast. Mount Rainier, Salton Sea, Salt Lake, and White Sands.
11. The design of the coffer in the King's Chamber, Great Pyramid of Giza, and a future event of great significance to the human race. This future event will be the Second Coming of Christ.

Sources For This Section

Charles Piazzi-Smyth, "Our Inheritance in the Great Pyramid." London: W. Isbister, 1880.

"McGraw-Hill Encyclopedia of Science and Technology." New York: McGraw-Hill, Vol. 12, 1960.

M.K. Jessup, "UFOs and the Bible." New York: Citadel Press, 1956.

Major Donald E. Keyhoe, "Flying Saucers Top Secret." New York: G.P. Putnam, 1960.

A FLYING SAUCER 15-YEAR SUMMARY

By George D. Fawcett

George D. Fawcett

(**A** summary of 15 years of investigation, study and research by Mr. George D. Fawcett, a native of Woburn, Massachusetts. Fawcett, the owner of the famed *"Saucerina Collection,"* is well-known for his illustrated UFO lectures, investigations and writings concerning flying saucers and other strange aerial phenomena. He is a member of NICAP and APRO and currently serves on the Interplanetary News Service Advisory Board. Mr. Fawcett is also the founder and president of the Massachusetts and Rhode Island Two-State UFO Study Group for Adults.)

It is only fitting that on the fifteenth anniversary of the first modern flying saucer scare, the UFO sightings by pilot Kenneth Arnold over Mount Rainier, Washington, on June 24, 1947, an up-to-date review be made of the situation today.

After 15 years of intense research and investigation into the strange aerial phenomena, which are still being reported worldwide, I am ready to re-affirm my own conclusions of 10 years ago, after five years of study and evaluation of the total UFO picture in recent years.

In 1952, my conclusions were not that the flying saucers are a real and ageless phenomenon, worldwide in extent. Not only did they give evidence of being extraterrestrial in origin and under intelligent control, but they also demonstrated periodic cycles of appearances and recorded landings throughout history. They also demonstrated the capability of hostile acts on many occasions. After reviewing the past 10 years, I am convinced, beyond the shadow of a doubt, that these conclusions are still valid today, as mankind approaches completion of its own first five years of space travel attempts.

In 1959, the United States Air Force concluded that the flying saucers are serious business, after telling the public that they didn't even exist for over 13 years officially.

Now in 1962, they have once again stated that these objects are nonexistent for the record.

What many people don't know is that, despite the fact that many of the top brains in the country are still striving to find a solution to the mystery of Unidentified Flying Objects, after 15 years the mystery is greater than ever.

What the Air Force is worried about is that these same UFOs have been responsible for the loss of many of our best planes and pilots. Also these objects have resulted in burns, electric shock and other injuries to numerous eyewitnesses.

Unofficially these incidents have already been documented and certified as authentic, but officially the Air Force, governed by the CIA's new releases on the UFO problem today, cannot admit these findings.

The evidence for the existence of these strange flying objects is overwhelming, and related to our national security. Officially recognition cannot be given to this subject, because the Air Force fears growing hysteria and the dangers of a serious panic, once these revelations are made known.

And most of all, strong recent demands for open hearings in Congress on the subject have caused the Air Force and CIA even greater concern. People are not about to accept their findings until their investigations can appeal to reason, not emotion. This accounts for the on-again, off-again news releases on UFOs to the general public, and this educational process may be the best way to handle the problem. But there are other problems besides hysteria and panic.

The dangers are increasing daily for UFO flights over the poles being mistaken for Russian or American-guided missiles and planes, thus possibly provoking an accidental World War III. False propaganda claims of secret weapons by an enemy could bring about chaos during a crisis.

Many defense personnel are concerned about radar pickups of UFOs, not to mention the many head-on passes and near collisions of UFOs with military and commercial airplanes.

Possible friendly space visitors to our world would be provoked to hostility because of firings upon them by pilots in the air and persons on the ground. These incidents may be the reasons for hostile acts by flying saucers already on record.

Many researchers are aware of a five-year cycle of UFO sightings. In 1942, these mysterious objects were seen in large numbers over Los Angeles; in 1947 came the Kenneth Arnold episode, in 1952 the Washington, D.C. radar pickups, and in 1957, demonstrations of electromagnetic interference on ignitions of cars and trucks in Texas and various foreign countries. In 1962, sightings rapidly built up, coming to a peak in December, in accordance with past performances. Besides the five-year cycle, Mars' opposition every 26 months has always resulted in large flurries of flying saucer sightings and bears a close watch again in 1963.

There are many handicaps in UFO investigation. Among these are: (1) official censorship through military orders; (2) ridicule through human nature's emotionalism; (3) false and fantastic claims by so-called contactees; (4) public and press apathy toward the subject; (5) reports by crackpots, religious cranks, publicity hounds, malicious practical jokers who reflect badly on the true version of flying saucers; and (6) fear of the unknown, panic and hysteria.

Today many scientists believe in UFOs.

A sober, scientific investigation of the phenomenon will not come until all nations have given recognition to the existence of flying saucers, which has only come from two or three countries. It will take international teamwork to establish a solution to the riddle of the flying saucers, perhaps even the establishment of the Interplanetary Geo-Physical Year study. General L.M. Chassin, Coordinator of the Air Defense for the Allied Air Forces (NATO), recently said, "I have asked that governments take the initiative, and instead of ridiculing saucer believers, set up commissions of inquiry in as many civilized countries as possible. We must become dedicated in our zeal that the consequences may be incalculable for the whole human race."

During the past 15 years I have spent much of my time, money and energy into the investigation of the flying saucers. I have noticed time and time again certain aspects of this phenomenon which repeat themselves over and over again. These repetitions indicate a real phenomenon, one that can be studied by both science and society. Already the UFOs have had their effects upon science, religion, history, philosophy, and many of the other aspects of day-to-day living. A study of the UFO quickly leads one to a study of mankind itself. And if God is the Creator, then he is identified with every part of his Creation, and that includes flying saucers also. The big question to the UFO mystery, therefore, is why are these things being seen in the skies worldwide? A new space philosophy should become the thing of the future.

Aspects of flying saucers that have been repeated often and are likely to reoccur at any time in the present are:

1. Sightings of UFOs that demonstrate superior speeds and maneuvers, beyond those of present satellites, aircraft and missiles.

2. Radar trackings of UFOs.

3. Photographs and movies of the objects.

4. Pursuits of UFOs by planes in the sky and by cars on open highways.

5. Falls of fragments and angel hair from UFOs.

6. Near collisions with planes and UFOs.

7. Physiological effects such as electric shock, radiation burns, temporary paralysis by observers in close encounters with UFOs.

8. Electromagnetic interference reports on planes, cars, lights, TV, motors and communication devices.

9. Sky-quakes and explosions in the skies during UFO appearances.

10. Sounds and smells attributed to UFOs.

11. Landings and near-landings of UFOs and their occupants.

12. Hostile acts due to UFOs.

13. Reports by so-called contactees.

At the present time, there is a growing battle between the Associated Press and United Press International news wires in reporting in detail dates, locations, descriptions, etc., of reported aerial phenomena. One can only guess as to why such leading magazines as True, Life and Look have reversed their old policies towards flying saucers. Each at first carried many saucer stories but now appears anti-saucer. Many articles are carried by local papers, never reaching the big newswires.

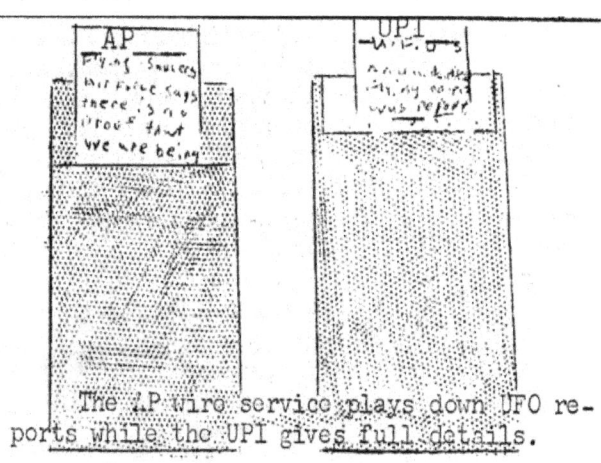

The AP wire service plays down UFO reports while the UPI gives full details.

Perhaps a metaphysical explanation will be applied to the UFO solution in the future. One thing, however, is sure: the unidentified flying objects (otherwise known as flying saucers) of the past and of the present, even after 15 years of hot controversy, are destined to remain with us in the future. I can draw no other sound conclusions. Can you?

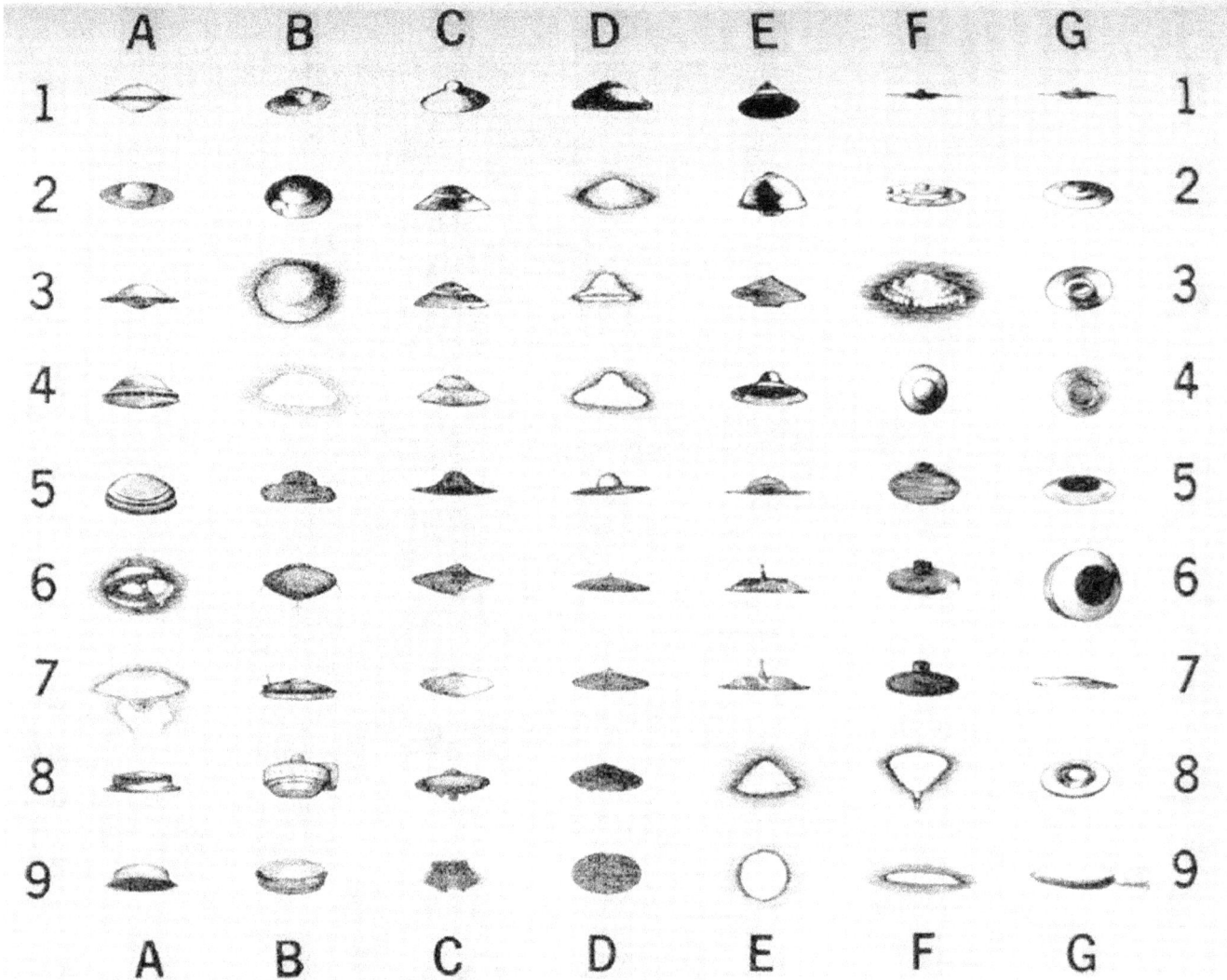

Chart of observed UFO Shapes.

Photo is from the 1965 Congress of Scientific Ufologists in Cleveland. (Left - Right): Dale Rettig, Gene Steinberg (in the third row back), Allen Greenfield and Rick Hilberg.

17-year-old David Halperin investigating the Glassboro, NJ, UFO "landing."

Timothy Green Beckley contemplates a portrait of Space Brother Orthon.

INSIDE THE SAUCERS - MR. UFOS TEENAGE YEARS

Timothy Green Beckley - UFO & Paranormal Pioneer

Timothy Green Beckley has been described as the Hunter Thompson of UFOlogy by the editor of UFO magazine Nancy Birnes.

Since an early age his life has more or less revolved around the paranormal.

At the age of three his life was saved by an invisible force. The house he was raised in was thought to be haunted. His grandfather saw a headless horseman.

Beckley also underwent out of body experiences starting at age six And saw his first of three UFOs when he was but ten, and has had two more sightings since – including an attempt to communicate with one of these objects.

Tim grew up listening to the only all night talk show in the country that revolved around the strange and unexplained. Long John Nebel's guests included the early UFO contactees who claimed to have visited other planets and built time machines in the desert. Tim was fascinated by everything that went bump in the night – or even in the daylight for that matter. Years later, Tim was to appear on Long John's show numerous times and over the years has been a frequent guest on hundreds of programs which have come and gone just like ghosts in the night. He si a popular guest on Coast to Coast AM. Has appeared on William Shatners Weird Or What? And an episode of UFO Hunters regarding the dreaded Men In Black. He has his own podcast, Unraveling The Secrets and MR UFOs Secret Files, a new YouTube channel.

Tim started his career as a writer early on – at age 14 he purchased a mimeograph machine and began to publish the Interplanetary News Service Report. Over the years he has written over 25 books on everything from rock music to the secret MJ12 papers. He has been a stringer for the national tabloids such as the Enquirer and editor of over 30 different magazines (most of which never lasted more than a couple of issues). His longest running effort was the newsstand publication *UFO UNIVERSE* which went for 11 years. Today he is the president of Inner Light/Global Communications and editor of the *Conspiracy Journal and Bizarre Bazaar*.

He is one of the few Americans ever to be invited to speak before closed door meetings on UFOs presided over by the late Earl of Clancarty at the House of Lords in England. He visited Loch Ness in Scotland while in the UK and went home with a belief that Nessie was somehow connected with dragons of mythology as well as strange discs engraved on cathedrals and ghostly phenomenon.

The Inner Light Publications and Global Communications' catalog of books and video titles now number over 200, including the works of Tim Swartz, Sean Casteel, Commander X, Brad Steiger, John Keel, Tracy Twyman, T. Lobsang Rampa and a host of many other authors.

INSIDE THE SAUCERS - MR. UFOS TEENAGE YEARS

He probably knows more about the history of the UFO movement since the early 1950s than anyone today. Because of his fair and balanced approach he made friends with everyone regardless of whether or not he believed their stories.

Tim has written over 30 books himself, and contributed to dozens more, including:

Our Alien Planet – This Eerie Earth

Strange Saga

Secret Prophecy of Fatima Revealed

Subterranean Worlds Inside Earth

The Truth About Crashed UFOs

UFOs Among The Stars (Celebrity encounters)

MJ-12 and The Riddle of Hangar 18

Nazi UFO Time Travelers

The Matrix Control System of Philip K. Dick And The Paranormal Synchronicities of Timothy Green Beckley

Tim is known among horror movie fans as Mr. Creepo. When asked his major cinema influences he mentions Nancy Reagan as having gotten him involved as a horror host. During the hay day of double features and Time Square grind houses he worked as a movie review critic as well as a publicist for several small film companies. His recent efforts include *Skin Eating Jungle Vampires* and *Blood Sucking Vampire Freaks*.

A young Timothy Green Beckley.

WE ACCEPT MONEY ORDERS · CHECKS · PAYPAL (mrufo8@hotmail.com) Credit Cards: 732-602-3407

REVEALED FOR THE FIRST TIME: THE TRUE IDENTITY OF THE MYSTERIOUS WHISTLE BLOWER KNOWN AS. . .

COMMANDER X
WILL THE REAL COMMANDER X PLEASE STAND UP!

NEW! – COMMANDER X FILES UPDATED

For more than a decade the mysterious Commander X has caused dissension among conspiracy theorists, Area 51 aficionados and UFO believers. Some accept his hair-raising accounts of working behind the scenes with the CIA, the NSA and other government and quasi-federal agencies at face value, while others scratch their heads in bewilderment and wonder if his first-hand chronicles cannot be linked to a disinformation program.

For the first time, here is the complete dossier on Commander X's many exploits both with various groups of highly aggressive ultra-terrestrials, as well as his battle with our own earthly authorities hell-bent on keeping these matters TOP SECRET! –

Included among the many shocking – and surprising – revelations in this book:

** The Alien Dinosaur Connection. – ** Who inhabits the Subterranean Regions of Earth? – ** Evidence suggests human victims were still alive, when their blood was drained and body parts removed in underground UFO bases. – ** The many special powers of ETs – including levitation, dematerialization, invisibility, mind control, advanced light beam technology. **A Nazi – Alien collaboration. How the Occult inner circle of the Third Reich contacted grey aliens before World War II using ritual magic. – ** Evidence Hitler shipped equipment and siave laborers to the Antarctic to construct a fleet of flying saucers. – ** Proof that the Nazis transferred into the midst of the American spy and space agencies.

AND MOST IMPORTANT OF ALL – ARE HUMAN CLONES GOING TO BE USED TO REPLACE ASSASSINATED POLITICIANS?

Only Commander X can dare answer these questions.
❏ Order THE COMMANDER X FILES - Large Format. 200+ Pages – $24.00.

❏ NEW! – AMERICA'S TOP SECRET TREATY WITH ALIEN LIFE FORMS
– PLUS THE HIDDEN HISTORY OF OUR TIME!

Is The "Treaty" A "False Flag?" – Or Some CIA Sponsored "Smoke Screen?" They arrived without our knowledge or consent and told our military leaders they came in peace for the benefit of humankind, and would gladly start an exchange program with the people of the planet earth which could lead to a "Golden Age." We wholeheartedly believed them and agreed to the "Treaty" almost without any sort of protest. Then they began to abduct our women! Then they returned for our children! Soon after they began to rape the earth's resources! And it became apparent they ultimately wanted to control our minds and capture our souls for their selfish reasons, some too horrific to comprehend.

And because they are too embarrassed to admit they went along with this Treaty, the U.S. government and the military industrial complex refuse to let the public know what has been going on for nearly half a century, keeping a tight lid on this Treaty and its various "exchange programs." But now there might be a ray of hope thanks to the whistle blower known as Commander X. This is your opportunity to find out about the "Treaty," and protect yourself and your loved ones from a possible "enemy attack" that could come out of the sky, as predicted by Nostradamus, as detailed in the Book of Revelations.

Find Out The Truth For Yourself by ordering SECRET TREATY WITH ALIENS.
❏ Large Format – 186 Pages – $20.00.

❏ **SPECIAL: BOTH NEW BOOKS BY COMMANDER X - $39.00 + $5 S/H**
TIMOTHY G. BECKLEY, BOX 753, NEW BRUNSWICK, NJ 08903

ALL TITLES AVAILABLE ON AMAZON.COM — PRINT AND KINDLE EDITIONS.

BEYOND ANYTHING YOU EVER THOUGHT WAS POSSIBLE

THE MATRIX CONTROL SYSTEM OF PHILIP K. DICK AND THE PARANORMAL SYNCHRONICITIES OF TIM BECKLEY

You Have Doubtlessly Seen The Movies Based Upon What We Have All Come to Believe Are Exceptionally Brilliant Science Fiction Novels Written By The Late Philip K. Dick
TOTAL RECALL—BLADE RUNNER—THE ADJUSTMENT BUREAU—MINORITY REPORT

But what you probably didn't know is that their creator was living out some of the same incredibly bizarre scenarios that he wrote about. One can easily compare Philip to the character played by Arnold Schwarzenegger in "Total Recall," who found himself in a parallel universe on a faraway planet, despite the fact that he was only supposed to be hooked up in a laboratory to a machine that creates realistic yet imaginary, dream-like images. For some reason, those that have implanted this "false memory" in his head want him dead. Which reality is the character really living in?

At a sci-fi press conference held in France in 1977, Philip tried to explain some of his bewildering thoughts about the existence of a parallel or self-contained – Matrix-like – universe created by "someone" who has the ability to alter the course of our reality for us:

"People claim to remember past lives," Philip told the throng of reporters. "I claim to remember a different – very different – present life. I know of nobody who has ever made this claim before but I rather suspect that my experience is not unique. What perhaps is unique is my willingness to talk about it. We are living in a computer-programmed reality and the only clue we have to it is when some variable is changed and some alteration in our reality occurs . . . and because of this a variable WAS changed – reprogrammed as it were – and an alternative world branched off."

The well-known collector of scientific curiosities, Charles Fort, is often quoted as having said: "The Earth is a farm. We are someone else's property." He likened our condition to being movable pieces on a chess board.

"There is no doubt that we are under some sort of surveillance and that an 'invisible hand' has the ability to carve out our existence and 'interfere' in our daily lives by creating a variety of bizarre 'play scripts' that to some may seem like pure 'coincidences.'" Or so says pop culture paranormalist Tim Beckley, who notes that "Synchronicities are not just random occurrences but are laid out before us by some sort of synchronicity command post, which ably demonstrates their mastery or control over us poor earthlings."

Drawing on the masterful mind of creative genius Philip K. Dick (some to this day perceive him to have been a total "mad man") we offer up dozens of his personal experiences, as well as those of others in the UFO and paranormal fields, where synchronicities seem to abound. Beckley and co-author Sean Casteel lay out a plausible scenario to "explain" the intricate workings of what has been dubbed "The Synchronicity Command Board," or "Earth Coincidence Control Office," as so aptly named by the brilliant American marine biologist and neurologist, Dr. John C. Lilly.

A titillating read that will challenge your concept of reality.

❏ **Order: "Philip K. Dick Synchronocities"**

**SPECIAL PRE PUBLICATION PRICE
—$15.95 + $5.00 S/H**
(Good till June 1, 2017, $18.95 thereafter).
Available by end of April, if not before!
**TIMOTHY G BECKLEY
BOX 753, NEW BRUNSWICK, NJ**
Credit Card 24/7 646 331-6777

PUBLISHING SINCE 1965 — OVER 250 "ORIGINAL" TITLES

Learn These Strange Oriental Secrets of Mind Reading
and Occult Mysteries!

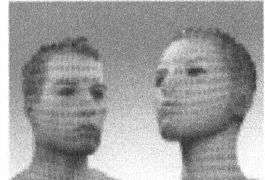

Issued By Occultists Dragonstar And S. Panehadaal, Here Are Long Hidden Secrets That Explain And Tell You How To Develope:

▲ Clairvoyance Of Present, Past and Future
▲ Premonitions ▲ Astral-body Traveling
▲ Psychometry, And Thought Transference.
▲ Clairaudience And Psychic Influence.
▲ Laws Of Psychic Attraction ▲ Crystal Gazing.
▲ Psychic And Magnetic Healing.

Teaches you how to develop a striking, dominating personality – you can use to enhance your psychic abilities and influence and command others.

Order: COMMAND OTHERS THROUGH THOUGHT TRANSFERENCE, *presented in workbook/studyguide form. Over 300 pages – just $24.00 + $5 S/H*

TIMOTHY G BECKLEY
BOX 753, NEW BRUNSWICK, NJ 08903

Subterraneans Kidnap Humans!
The DERO COULD BE OUT TO GET YOU!

True Story Of Richard Shaver And His Conflict With The Evil Inner Earth Dwellers, Here Are Tales Of The Dero, Their Madness, Their Sadistic Abductions, And Their Sexually Twisted Perversions. Shaver exposed the Dero's attempts to murder, cause disasters and wars back in the 1940s in a series of articles in a national magazine. Thousands testified with their own experiences verifying that what he said was for real.

❏ **Order the: HIDDEN WORLDS –**

6 Volumes In The Series Available Now. Over 1200 Pages Printed In Large Format Editions. A virtual encyclopedia of these underground denizens and a few of the "good guys!" – **$99.00 + $8 S/H**

FREE: SHAVER'S CHILLING TALES FROM THE INNER EARTH – Companion Volume, 206 Pages, When Ordering Now.

TIMOTHY G BECKLEY
BOX 753, NEW BRUNSWICK, NJ 08903

Thousands Of People Vanish Every Year

IS THERE A UFO BASE IN THE BERMUDA TRIANGLE?

They walk out the door and are never seen again. They take a leisurely stroll along a forest trail and poof they are gone. They go on a cruise inside the Devil's Sea or Bermuda Triangle and the ship they are on is either never seen again or it is found without passengers and crew weeks later in a far distant part of the ocean.

The 747 disappears from radar and does not seem to have crashed, yet no bodies or wreckage are ever recovered?

Many strange explanations have been offered: Worm Holes. UFOs. Criptids. Bizarre Woodland "Wild Men." Magnetic Force Fields. God's Rapture. The Dero. Earth Elementals. But does anyone have the answer? If you have read any of the books in the "411 Series," or are a fan of Charles Fort, John Keel or Frank Edwards you will want to read ❏ **MYSTERIOUS DISAPPEARANCES: THEY NEVER CAME BACK.** Large Format. 288 Pages. $21.95 + $5.00 S/H

TIMOTHY G BECKLEY
BOX 753, NEW BRUNSWICK, NJ 08903

DID JESUS WALK AMONG THE INDIANS?

JOIN THE SEARCH FOR THE PALE PROPHET IN THE AMERICAS

Sean Casteel asks: "Who was the mysterious robe-clad healer who walked among the tribes of the Americas almost two thousand years ago? Was he the Messiah on a God-given mission to bring peace and compassion to uncharted, far-away lands...or possibly a representative of an "Ancient Alien" group on an off-world assignment?" Based upon Sean's research and the works of the late L. Taylor Hansen.
❏ **SEARCH FOR THE PALE PROPHET—$18 + $5 S/H**

Also Of Interest – ❏ FLYING SAUCERS IN THE HOLY BIBLE. ❏ ARK OF THE COVENANT AND OTHER SECRET WEAPONS OF THE ANCIENTS. ❏ SECRET PROPHECY OF FATIMA REVEALED

($18 Each – All 4 titles this ad **$55.00 + $7 S/H**)

TIMOTHY G BECKLEY
BOX 753, NEW BRUNSWICK, NJ 08903

Inner Light – Global Communications

P.O. Box 753

New Brunswick, NJ 08903

www.conspiracyjournal.com

mrufo8@hotmail.com

Mr. UFOs Secret Files – YouTube

https://www.youtube.com/user/MRUFO1100

www.ingramcontent.com/pod-product-compliance
Lightning Source LLC
Chambersburg PA
CBHW081324040426
42453CB00013B/2295